D1125016

'I had stopped before, but had returned to smoking as a direct result of playing a character on stage who smoked. I was using herbal cigarettes in the play, but the process of smoking them rekindled the smoker in me, and after a few months, I succumbed to real cigarettes. Gillian Riley's technique made the crucial difference this time. It has now been nearly three and a half years since I smoked a real cigarette. This includes a seven month run of a play in which I had, once again, to smoke herbals repeatedly, but this time I managed to stay smoke-free.

In my experience, Gillian Riley's method is the only one (of many I have encountered) that really gets to the heart of the addiction and roots it out. I feel so much better for not smoking, and have gained no weight as a result. I'd strongly recommend her technique to anyone who is serious about getting free of this addiction.'

Juliet Stevenson, actress

'To say I was pessimistic about my chances is putting it mildly - I thought I'd be the last man on earth to be able to stop smoking. I had tried in vain to quit a few times until I finally stopped in the summer of 1997 with the guidance of Gillian Riley.

What made the difference this time was understanding that I had a choice. The big mistake is that people try to stop smoking by telling themselves it's horrible and they mustn't do it. This makes quitting a difficult and miserable business. Many smokers are rebels by nature and it's no good telling rebels that they can't do something – nothing makes them want to smoke more. But give them their own choice and they find it very much easier.

I feel proud of the fact that I haven't smoked for six years and don't miss it one bit. When you achieve something like this, which you never imagined possible, it has a positive effect on almost every aspect of your life.'

Mark Knopfler, musician

'I have done very well since attending Gillian's overeating course. The main achievement is that I no longer diet, and this fact alone has had the most positive effect on my eating habits. I no longer think about food so much, I'm no longer obsessive about my weight, I hardly ever binge, and never before has my weight been so under control. I had always believed that dieting was counter-productive, but your course helped to consolidate that fact.

I still enjoy my food and look forward to indulging myself with the odd treat, but I very rarely now eat between meals and usually just have one smallish course for dinner in the evening. The important thing is I have no anxieties about ballooning to massive proportions because I know now that this will not happen.

I could say so much more. This approach is absolutely on the right track and I'm very pleased to have discovered it.'

Eve Harrison, Oxfordshire

'*Willpower!* has given me much to think about and ponder on. I have taken a long, hard look at many aspects of my life and have made real progress on raising my self-esteem and changing the way I think, especially about having choices.

This has already had a profound effect on my life. I had a very difficult meeting recently with an ex-boyfriend, and I was totally dreading that I would get into a state, say the wrong thing, end up in tears and find that everything had disintegrated around me again. But knowing it was my choice to act in these ways or to be calm and collected changed everything. It gave me so much confidence. At the end of the discussion I was a little tearful, but I had said what I wanted to say and now feel I can move my life on again, as indeed I have. This is my choice. I can use my willpower to make positive changes in my life and this has been something I have been able to do quietly and privately.

This book has helped me turn my thoughts upside down, made me see things differently and started me on a new path of thinking that has already enriched my life.'

Kate Morris, Stamford

WILLPOWER!

GILLIAN RILEY

Vermilion
LONDON

1 3 5 7 9 10 8 6 4 2

Text © 2003 Gillian Riley
Illustration © 2003 Beth Higgins

Gillian Riley has asserted her right to be identified as the author
of this work under the Copyright, Designs and Patents Act 1988.

All rights reserved. No part of this publication may be reproduced,
stored in a retrieval system, or transmitted in any form or by any
means, electronic, mechanical, photocopying, recording or otherwise
without the prior permission of the copyright owners.

First published in the United Kingdom in 2003 by
Vermilion, an imprint of Ebury Press
Random House UK Ltd
Random House, 20 Vauxhall Bridge Road, London SW1V 2SA

Random House Australia (Pty) Limited
20 Alfred Street, Milsons Point, Sydney,
New South Wales 2061, Australia

Random House New Zealand Limited
18 Poland Road, Glenfield,
Auckland 10, New Zealand

Random House (Pty) Limited
Endulini, 5A Jubilee Road, Parktown 2193, South Africa

The Random House Group Limited Reg. No. 954009
www.randomhouse.co.uk
Papers used by Vermilion are natural, recyclable products
made from wood grown in sustainable forests.

A CIP catalogue record for this book is available from the British Library.

ISBN 0091887690

Printed and bound in Great Britain by
Mackays of Chatham Ltd, Chatham, Kent

Typset by seagulls

The clients' stories at the ends of Chapters Six and Seven first
appeared in an article in the journal *The Therapist* (4:4, 1997).

CONTENTS

to Seven with love

CHAPTER ONE

Introducing Willpower

What to use willpower for and how to get started

Sometimes people find themselves at a point in their lives when they feel held back, as if they are living in a world that is limiting and confining them in some way. They try changing things – the colour of their hair, their job, a friendship or place to live – in the hope that this will make all the difference, but they know somehow that nothing has really changed at all. The wallpaper is a different colour, but they're still just as stuck inside.

If this is something you can identify with, even just a bit, maybe the change that will really make the difference is going to require willpower.

You might have tried resigning yourself to the way things are, but my guess is you're reading this book because you're not happy with that. You know what this is really about and you know it's never going to go away by itself. You know you are compromising, settling for a limited version of who you are. Perhaps you also know that even beginning to set your sights on a challenge starts to break you out of that mould.

This is what this book is all about. It's about making those changes you want to make – and making them last. It's about taking control of some area of your life, so that you can become more like the person you really want to be. It's about living in a way that more fully reflects your true self. It's about discovering that willpower isn't something that gets handed out to some and not to others, but that it's a skill you can develop through understanding and practice.

The amazing truth, you see, is that when you do start to use your willpower, this can be one of the most liberating, exciting and rewarding things you will ever do. In a sense, it may not even matter all that much what you direct the power of your will towards. Facing any willpower challenge opens up endless possibilities in unlimited directions, simply because you develop greater trust in and a more positive regard for yourself. It introduces a stronger sense of purpose and hope into your life, and that's something you can build on to get to where you want to be.

A good place to start is to consider that you already have willpower. Everybody does. All you need to do is learn how to use it. How to access it. How to unlock its potential.

The Power of Your Will

The dictionary tells me that will is 'the attitude of the mind which is directed with conscious attention to some action'. Then it says that will is the way someone decides on what action to take, adding words such as 'free will', 'purpose' and 'determination'. Our will is our ability to choose, either to carry out actions we want to take or not to do things we don't want to do.

Picking up your hand and placing a finger on the end of your nose is an act of will. If you do it you'll notice that the conscious attention of your mind directs that action. But let's face it, using your will to put your finger on your nose is not likely to be the reason you're reading this book. The point of the word 'power' is to accomplish far more challenging acts of will. We need to add *power* to our will when we are facing actions that involve:

★ **Acting on impulse** – One reason we find it tough to direct our will is precisely because it requires conscious attention. It's so easy to get distracted by all that's going on in our lives that we often act on impulse, only regretting later that we lack the willpower to change our ways.

★ **Fear** – Whether you fear failure or maybe fear unknown outcomes, you begin any struggle with will in a more pessimistic frame of mind. This undermines willpower because you're less likely to put in the amount of effort that's needed when you're not all that confident of your goal.

★ **Perseverance** – Using willpower doesn't usually involve a single choice but a series of seemingly endless acts of will. Maybe each one choice isn't too daunting – it's choice number 3,825 that does you in! Just the thought of the perseverance you'll need could deter you from even making a start.

★ **Delayed rewards** – When your rewards aren't immediate it seems at first that whatever choice you make is a bad one. You hope something good will come out of it at some point but you have little or no evidence of it in the present time. The more delayed the rewards, the more of a challenge it is to use willpower.

★ **Addiction** – A very particular challenge for our will, addiction means that at the same time as wanting to control our addiction, we are also attracted to it. Not only that, but addiction means we will encounter the difficulty of withdrawal whenever we try to take control. Both of these elements place us in a state of conflict and, combined with the previous four points, make tackling addiction the biggest willpower challenge of them all.

No matter what it is you want to use willpower for, understanding these five themes will make all the difference, so we'll be looking at them throughout this book. We'll see that although these issues can make it difficult to use willpower, each one can be handled in positive and effective ways. They are blocks to using willpower – but they can also be your routes to success. It's precisely through understanding them that you gain a greater degree of mastery in your life and widen the opportunities available to you.

Maybe using willpower for you means getting out of a relationship that is destructive and holds you back. It might mean quitting that job you hate even though you're not sure what you'll do next. Perhaps you'd like the willpower to introduce yourself to someone you're attracted to. Or it might mean talking less when you're nervous and don't stop talking, and the next day you wish you hadn't been like that. You could want willpower so you can stick to an exercise routine. Maybe the fear of public speaking is your challenge. It was for me and I'll tell you about that later.

These are examples of how you might want some power behind your will, but we will spend much more time on how to access willpower to take control of an addiction. This is, of course, about using willpower *not* to take some actions. The list of things people can get addicted to is a very long one. More common examples would include smoking, alcohol, caffeine, shopping, gambling, different kinds of drugs and overeating (especially sugar and wheat).

Some kinds of relationships, and sex itself, can be thought of as addictive as well.

Addiction is best described in terms of actions you take over and over again that you have real difficulty controlling, even though you want to. You think, at least sometimes, that you'd like to stop doing it or do it less often, but it doesn't turn out that way. Sometimes you can gain control for a while, but you find it tough to keep it up for very long. Sometimes when you try to cut it out, you end up doing it even more.

In learning how to develop willpower to take control of addiction, we will mostly look at examples of quitting smoking and taking control of overeating. These are the areas I have the most experience with, both through my own personal experience and through more than two decades of leading courses and counselling. I can give you examples and explain strategies that I've seen a great many different people employ. I know what works and I know where people get blocked in the use of will – and what needs to be done to remove those blocks.

Willpower and Addiction

I suspect that smoking and overeating are what most people would like to develop willpower for. For many people they are by far the greatest challenge and are often thought to be the most difficult behaviours to change in a lasting way. So, if you can understand something about how to develop long-term willpower in these areas, anything else should be a breeze in comparison!

In case you're wondering if you are addicted in the first place, there's no precise scientific definition. For example, it's well established that the nicotine in tobacco is behind one of the most powerful addictions of all, but there are people who smoke just a few cigarettes every now and then. It is said that only 5 per cent continue to smoke very occasionally, but the question is, at what point could we describe them as addicted? One cigarette a month? One a week? One a day? One an hour? The fact is that this is impossible to say; there's no place where anyone can draw a line to say *exactly* where addiction begins. Most smokers, though, know very well when they have become addicted. Then, the question is how to quit.

Often, people try to take control of addictions in more or less the same way they would face any other kind of challenge. This is a big mistake. There are common themes, but there are also very important differences. There are very particular elements that make up an addiction, and this means you need to take a completely different approach.

Let's see what some of these differences are, so that as we proceed we can understand more clearly how to build willpower in order to overcome addiction.

Do you feel inspired?

As you may know, willpower can be effortless when you are passionate and single-minded about what you want to do. Even in the face of fear and setbacks, a passion for your ultimate goal will carry you through. Any time you meet an obstacle, you remind yourself of what you are aiming for and you get back on course.

However, when dealing with addiction, many people think they're supposed to feel inspired, so they wait until they feel some real excitement about using willpower to take control. This is the worst thing you can do. The whole nature of addiction creates ambivalence, fear and doubt, so that you think you should stop doing it, while at the same time you don't really want to – at least, not right now! It will be a huge step if you can accept that you may not feel all that inspired to begin with, and go ahead anyway. At best, you might get fleeting glimpses of excitement at the prospect of taking control of an addiction. This is a good sign, but don't expect much more than that.

A great many smokers tell themselves that they'll become inspired to quit as soon as any serious health problem shows up. But studies of smokers who have had serious problems show that in most cases this doesn't actually happen.[1] As many as 80 per cent of smokers who have a heart attack either don't stop at all or take it up again soon after. In fact, serious health problems can make it even more difficult for smokers to quit successfully, for reasons we'll look at later.

People spend their whole lives smoking and overeating, waiting for inspiration to change that never happens. Even when inspiration does strike it's impossible to sustain – *and it's precisely when the passion has disappeared from view that the addictive behaviour is likely to re-establish itself*. The real skill is to use willpower even though you're not feeling particularly inspired.

Are other people involved?

Is anyone else involved in what you are setting out to do, and does your success depend on their cooperation? There's nothing like getting people to work together towards a common goal. Collective will is an exceptional force, and developing good communication with these other people and staying in communication with them is going to be an essential part of the process. Without communication – and lots of it – success is unlikely.

However, when dealing with addiction, one of the most common mistakes is to try to get other people involved. Often, this is just an attempt to get other people to do the willpower bit for you. Not only is that impossible, but it means you're still not using your own willpower yourself, and that's not likely to work in the longer term. When it comes to dealing with addiction, nobody else can do it for you, so by far the best strategy is to learn how to use your willpower by yourself.

To realise that your willpower is yours alone, that it belongs to nobody else and doesn't rely on anyone else is extremely liberating and empowering. The way you make this a reality is not to talk about it at all with the people in your life. Taking control of addiction is all about how you communicate with yourself. Keep what you are doing private and you keep it where it belongs.

There's one exception to this, and that is if you join a group or see a counsellor for support in overcoming an addiction. What makes this an exception is that you discuss things in the group or counselling sessions, but when you're actually using willpower to control yourself, you'll be out there in your own life. You could be on your own or at social events with friends or family. There you are, thinking about smoking a cigarette or having a second helping at dinner. Those are the moments when you would want to use willpower and those are the moments when your best strategy is to do that privately. If the people in your life don't know what you're up to, they aren't likely to try to get involved. As you may already know, other people trying to influence your will in these matters is often a sure route to disaster.

Are you trying to control too much?

You probably know the saying: when life sends you lemons, make lemonade. But what if life sends you apples? If you've committed yourself to making lemonade you'll be pitting your will against an inescapable fact of life. You'll be banging your head against a brick wall, and this is never a wise thing to do. If you continue to insist on making lemonade you'll get worn down and driven crazy, when all you need to do is simply switch your sights towards apple juice.

If what you are attempting to create isn't working, this could be crucial feedback that this is not the right path for you. It's important to pay attention to this because there are times and situations when your will is not the issue. This is because there are limits, there are things outside of you and your will, not least of which is the will of others. For example, you might be pursuing a love interest who isn't interested in you. You might be seeking work in a career that's not right for you.

Sometimes simply deciding to pursue a certain goal begins to open doors and deliver magic results. But sometimes it doesn't. Sometimes there's a huge 'NO WAY!' coming back at you and nothing is happening the way you planned. There's always a dance between what we aim for and what life is going to deliver, no matter what we do. We can only push so far, and some aspects of our goal might always be beyond our control.

I don't want to discourage you from trying. Making an attempt can be important because you may only find these things out once you've put in a real bit of effort. And you can say that at least you tried, and that will be something.

Maybe it's time to let go a bit, to turn and follow a different path or to stop insisting on some particular details. Maybe you can get what you want but not in exactly the way you wanted it. Maybe you're feeling frustrated and running out of patience, and all you need to do is take a break and do something else for a while. Come back to it later and you're likely to feel more refreshed and positive about it.

However, when dealing with addiction, trying to reach compromises gets you into big trouble, and it's precisely when things get tough that it's best to stay in control. This is because anyone addicted has already developed very familiar, well-rehearsed and well-established ways of justifying their behaviour. For reasons we'll look at later, these justifications often seem entirely valid and based on trustworthy intuition. This is a major part of what makes addiction so tough to overcome. This addictive thinking convinces you that you can compromise – by only smoking roll-ups, or only gambling on the first Wednesday of the month, or by eating the biscuits and going for a longer run the next day. Most of all, addiction means you'll try to compromise by waiting for a better time to start to apply willpower.

Addiction, almost by definition, appears to enhance and support your life when in fact it doesn't. So those who are addicted will always seek out excuses, looking for any signs that this isn't the right time to take control. It's part of what addiction is all about. It will always seem sensible to wait for a better time to start using willpower, a time when there are no upsets, no distractions, no temptations and no stress. In other words – never!

Are you visualising success?

Visualisation is a widely used motivational tool, and it can be helpful with many challenges, such as public speaking or job interviews. Whatever you are setting out to accomplish, rehearse it over and over in your imagination. Then, when you do it in real life, you're more familiar with it because in a sense you've already been through it.

However, when dealing with addiction, the problem is that it involves *not* doing something. You know what would happen if I told you *not* to think about a green elephant? How can you not think about a green elephant when the image is right there in front of you? Instructing a smoker not to think about smoking or an overeater not to think about chocolate biscuits is very likely to create a similar, not too helpful effect.

Not only that, but it's possible you identify quite strongly with your addiction, so that it has become a part of your self-image. I've heard a great many people say they think of themselves as born smokers. Of course they aren't, but this is their way of describing their sense that smoking seems to be at the very core of their being. For them, trying to visualise not smoking is a very tall order. As I once heard on a relaxation tape for quitting smoking, they can see themselves sitting on a beach, feeling very relaxed, breathing deeply, watching the sun go down…but there's a cigarette burning away in their fingers. This, of course, can be hugely discouraging.

When it comes to using willpower with food, you might try to motivate yourself by visualising how slim you're going to be. This too can be unhelpful as it keeps you attached to weight loss as your goal, rather than the real cause of your problem, which is eating too much of the wrong things. Excess weight is simply one of the consequences of this, and, as with most problems in life, it's far better to deal with the cause of it than the effects. More on this later.

Are you taking on too much?

Many people these days try to pack much too much into their lives, and the last thing I'm going to do is to encourage you to do even more. If your life doesn't already include space for you to 'stop to smell the roses' then developing willpower to take on more will not only be unwise but probably ineffective. Maybe the best thing you can do is to develop the willpower to say no more often, to see the value in slowing down and easing up. This is especially relevant if you are already stressed or unwell in some way.

However, when dealing with addiction, this is rarely good

advice. Especially if you are stressed or unwell, it's all the more important to tackle your addictive behaviour. Excuses such as 'I don't have time' and 'I smoke/eat to cope with stress' are exactly what keep people smoking and overeating. The truth is that quitting smoking and/or cutting down on addictive overeating bring down levels of stress – provided they are handled correctly. Excuses can always be found but are only valid in fairly exceptional and temporary circumstances, such as a recent bereavement.

Are you sure it's your problem?

It's important to check that what you are setting out to do really is your problem and really is within your power to change. Are you aiming to exert your willpower over someone else? It might be that you are fed up with a situation you can do nothing to change and no amount of willpower will make any difference.

However, dealing with addiction is entirely within your control and not in the least bit dependent on anyone or anything else. This is the really good news! Unless, of course, you're wanting to change someone else's addictive behaviour, a child or partner, for example, which is very tough, if not impossible, to pull off. You can only go so far with that because you come up against the will of that other person. What often happens is that the more you try to control or influence them the more resistant and rebellious they become, so it can be extremely counter-productive.

Addiction is surely the number one challenge for willpower. It's also the most rewarding to overcome and for a great many people makes the crucial difference in their lives that absolutely nothing else – not money nor fame nor any other kind of success – will bring. In fact, it can sometimes be these kinds of successes that get people to see just how important willpower over addiction really is. No matter what you accomplish, no matter what joy life brings, failing in willpower, even in just one or two areas, can make it mean less. On the other hand, success with willpower can bring you a confidence and peace with yourself in a way that nothing else ever can.

The powerful connection between willpower and self-esteem is what we will explore further in our next chapter.

Step by Step

★ **Use this book and you'll get results** – These sections at the end of each chapter will point you in various directions, with very practical, step-by-step advice. You might want to create a journal to make notes about your insights and experiences as you go through this book. You might want to select a few phrases that stand out to you, write them on Post-it notes and put them up in your room to remind you of key ideas. It's likely you'll want to read at least parts of this book more than once. Some chapters will make much more sense the second time, when you look at them again having read the whole book.

★ **Identify your goals** – Make a note of the areas in your life where you want to develop willpower. Try to identify ways to use your willpower that will challenge you. See if you can find a sense of 'if only I could do *that*…anything would be possible'. Then you know you've got a goal that will bring fantastic rewards in your life, a goal that's worth a bit of a struggle.

★ **Identify fear** – Some degree of fear about what you want to accomplish is a very good sign because it shows you're on the right track. It means that what you're about to do is important to you, that it matters. Good. I hope it does matter! One problem, though, is that fear isn't always easy to spot because it can show up in disguise. Fear can show up in the guise of losing sight of your motivation, when you forget why you're bothering in the first place or why it's so important to you. It can show up as indifference and apathy, when you just keep talking yourself out of making any significant changes at all. You might not know this is fear because you never get far enough to feel it. You just stay safe, sort of secure and comfortable in familiar surroundings. You think you *should* do something about it one day, but the fear keeps you stuck so you never get close to actually doing anything about it.

★ **Accept fear as part of the process** – Some people assume they should feel confident of success to start with – but finding a goal to aim towards never provides you with a guarantee you'll reach it. There will always be uncertainty, no matter what you are hoping to achieve. You can never know for sure how it will all turn out, so it's inevitable that you will experience some fear. It may help you to remember that fear is an emotion closely linked to excitement. Think about watching a film that's a thriller, where you care about the leading characters, or watching some kind of sports event where you care about who wins. There's the fear of failure hand in hand with the excitement that keeps you involved. That's why it's fun. That's why you don't tell people the ending of a mystery thriller, because not knowing how it will end is a big part of what makes it interesting. It's a crucial part of life and something we often take for granted. Can we begin to imagine what it would be like if we knew exactly what will happen every day for the rest of our lives? There are degrees of fear, though, and although some fear is inevitable it is important to make it more reasonable and acceptable than sheer panic and hysteria. You'll see more as we go on that will bring down higher levels of fear and anxiety to a more manageable level.

★ **Describe overeating (eating more food than your body needs) as an addiction** – This is not to pass judgement but to help you to understand better the process of taking control. Many overeaters reason that they just happen to enjoy their food a lot. But take a look, for example, at celebrity chefs, who have amazing passion for food but aren't necessarily addictive overeaters. The difficulty in seeing overeating as an addiction arises partly because it has become so common in our culture; it just seems so normal.

★ **Read food labels** – If you find it tough to think of food as an addiction, consider that in Britain it is estimated that on average each person eats 1.25 lb of sugar every week, none of which is necessary for our nutritional needs. This is considered to be one of the most significant factors in the rise of obesity and related diseases, not to mention our consumption of processed wheat, which is pretty much the same as sugar as far as our bodies are concerned. Much of the sugar is 'hidden' in most commercially produced food. It's added by the manufacturers because it's addictive and therefore sells more of the product.

★ **Pay attention to what happens when you try to use willpower** – Reading this book could be an example, so notice your reactions and the choices you make as you go. Notice, for example, that you have the option of reading the words but not letting them sink in. Notice if you put the book down at some point and feel reluctant to return to it. If that happens, discover the block you encountered. Was it fear? ('I don't understand this bit, so I'm sure to fail.') Was it hopelessness? ('I'll never be able to keep it up.') Was it indifference? ('It's too much trouble.') When you discover what blocks your willpower, you can begin to overcome it. *And* you don't need to understand all of it for it to make a difference.

Where There's a Will: Gillian

At the end of each chapter you'll find contributions from different people about their experiences of willpower, and what it was that made the difference for them in breaking free from addictive behaviour. First, though, I'd like to tell you about willpower in terms of facing a fear. This is my story.

This particular challenge appeared in my life when I was about thirty, and had just attended a series of seminars where I learned how to stop smoking. It was a crucial moment in my life, not just because I had quit smoking but because I knew then that I wanted to teach others how to stop. I thought that if I could just help one person to stop smoking who wouldn't otherwise have been able to, that would be the most wonderful achievement. That's how I viewed it at the time and that's what inspired me.

There was one problem, though, and for me it was a

massive one. At some point I would be leading the seminars, standing up in front of people, thinking on my feet and answering questions. I would need to deal with people who were upset, confused, resistant, sceptical, fearful and even hostile. Most of all, I needed to be able to express myself clearly and with complete confidence in front of a group of people, perhaps twenty or fifty or more.

For me, this was a far greater challenge than anything I had ever faced in my life, and I think have ever faced since. At that time, put me in front of a group of people, no matter how small, no matter how friendly, no matter how supportive, and my knees would turn to jelly, the insides of my stomach would wobble and flop, my whole body would go hot and cold, and worst of all, my mind would go totally blank. My fear of talking rubbish and of being rejected was so great that the fear became a certainty. Even if I had uttered the wisest words in the universe, my message was 'I'm a complete idiot and a waste of your time. I'm very sorry I exist and I'm sorry for bothering you.' Get smokers to quit? I don't think so.

There was no reliable formula to take me forward. All I could do was search around, which I did for about a year, trying anything I could find to help me to overcome my fear of public speaking. I attended some courses. I discovered a public speaking coach and worked with her for a few months. Opportunities to practise were hard to come by, so I tried singing in a local bar. This was utterly terrifying, but it was a stepping stone because it had some degree of safety in it. If I knew a song well enough my mind could go blank and I'd still make it through on automatic. Songs only last a minute or two, so the agony wouldn't go on too long. And I was just about prepared to live with the possible failure of a flat note, a forgotten line or a disinterested audience.

Over that year, I willed myself to continue to get up in front of people whenever the opportunity arose. I certainly had some disasters, but my vision of what might become possible kept me going. The self-esteem and self-confidence I got from overcoming my biggest fear mean so much more to me than just having a skill in public speaking. Even if I never lead a course again or get up on a stage or appear on TV, I know that I can set what was for me an extraordinary goal, work towards it and achieve it.

I know that overcoming a fear such as this is not an unusual story and that these things happen in the lives of a great many people. You may know people who have faced similar fears and you may have a story like this to tell yourself. You may know as well as I do that when you feel strongly enough about what you're aiming for, things can be very straightforward and things you would never have dreamt of doing before become possible.

Notes

1. 'Some studies have actually found that patients with smoking-related diseases are less successful at stopping smoking than other types of hospital patients.' Nicotine Addiction in Britain, Report of the Tobacco Advisory Group of the Royal College of Physicians, 2000.

CHAPTER TWO

Your Own Best Friend

The connection between willpower and self-esteem

Imagine, if you will, that you've got the day off work, and that two very different friends have invited you to spend the day with them. It isn't possible to be with both, so you need to choose to spend this day with one or the other.

The first of these friends likes you and obviously enjoys your company. They often comment on things you're good at, and encourage you when things go well for you. They say things like 'You deserve that success – you worked hard for it.' They can see there are things you're not so good at, but love you anyway and accept that for everyone there's always room for improvement. They are honest and you know you can trust them to keep their word.

The other friend, as I said, is very different. They often

criticise you and predict failure at anything you attempt. No matter what you accomplish, they never fail to point out the one detail that could have been better. They say things like 'You'll manage to screw that up somehow, just like you did last time.' They lie to you often and are generally unreliable, making promises that are regularly broken.

My question to you is this: with everything else being equal, which friend do you prefer to spend this day with? If you answer 'the second', I'd better tell you right now that you're reading the wrong book! If you answer 'the first', let me explain the point of this exercise.

You see, I'm thinking of these friends as the thoughts you have inside your own head, the thoughts that – whether you like it or not – make up the continuous running commentary on your life, about how well you are performing and whether or not you 'make the grade'. Since this friend is one you'll spend not only your day off with, but every single one of your days, this running commentary has an enormous impact on the whole of your life.

My point is simple. Most people, given the chance, would prefer to think in ways that leave them more confident, relaxed, secure, positive and optimistic. But there's the catch: given the chance.

It could be that you've never really been given the chance. You may not have been given the chance if you were raised by a critical parent. Siblings, friends and teachers can leave their mark as well, and this is simply because every child learns about life by imitating whomever they are around. Everything – from how to button up a shirt to how to speak and write – is learned by copying others. We learn self-criticism from those who criticise us, just like we learn everything else. So if the message you hear is that you're not good enough, that you are somehow flawed and inadequate, lower self-esteem is the inevitable result.

Willpower and Self-Esteem

If you're beginning to wonder what all this has to do with willpower, the answer is: everything. Self-esteem and will-power go hand in hand. They're not exactly the same thing but they are very powerfully connected:

★ The lower your self-esteem, the less likely you are to use willpower because you'll tend to assume you will fail. You can't imagine yourself succeeding, *so you don't even try*.

★ The lower your self-esteem, the more you feel like you don't deserve to succeed at anything really important. Success may even feel strange, as if there's something wrong with it, so using willpower is less likely to last. Failure, on the other hand, feels familiar and comfortable.

★ Lower self-esteem makes the risk of attempting a willpower challenge even riskier, because failing can feel so deeply painful and even shameful. Mistakes and shortcomings can be more upsetting and feel more demoralising to those with lower self-esteem. Of course the pain of some failures is inevitable, but many can be overcome in a far more light-hearted manner, and this opens up the possibility of trying again. If even small failures lead to intense self-loathing and despair, there's a big incentive to stay safe and stick to what you know. Using willpower to make significant lifestyle changes may seem too big a risk to even consider.

★ Those with low self-esteem are often not all that interested in using willpower until serious ill health knocks them out of this complacency. Then they begin to fear worsening health, disability, pain and even death, and that's obviously extremely threatening motivation. Fear alone is not the best foundation on which to build willpower.

The big problem with low self-esteem is that it becomes a self-fulfilling prophecy. The sense that you're not good enough is projected on to everything you attempt and reinforced at every hurdle. It makes no sense at all to try harder if you're convinced you're going to fail anyway. So, you don't try any-where near hard enough or persist for anything like long enough – resulting in the failure you predicted in the first place!

For those with more fragile self-esteem, failure with

willpower is excellent ammunition for their self-critic. Whenever you drop out on willpower there's always some undeniable evidence in your life to remind you, and, of course, the well-rehearsed self-critic uses this as more proof that there's something terribly wrong with you. This evidence could be any number of things: smoking, overeating, excess weight, drinking too much, using drugs, debt – or all of the above! Thus, a belief that you don't have any willpower is forever bound up in the belief that you are seriously flawed.

It can become even more visible evidence when real success has been achieved in some particular area. A common example is the high-flier with a successful career, wonderful family life and good friends, who overeats and smokes and can't begin to take control of either problem. Many people try to compensate for low self-esteem by driving themselves to higher and higher achievements. It's their attempt to prove their worth – in business, family life and education. Often such people are puzzled by how they can be so effective and productive in so many ways, yet fail so miserably with willpower and addiction. The answer lies in their low self-esteem, which can remain unaffected by worldly success and still insists on expressing itself somehow.

Low self-esteem isn't necessarily a permanent state, though. Self-esteem varies from day to day, even from hour to hour. You might think of yourself as someone with fairly good self-esteem in general, but everyone's self-esteem takes a knock from time to time. At those times there's a real danger that you'll forget all about willpower. It may only last a day or two but that's the time when you're most likely to fall into more self-destructive behaviour by relapsing, bingeing or whatever.

For others, though, a lack of willpower is central to the ongoing theme of their lives, a low self-esteem theme that runs through relationships, career and practically everything else they turn themselves to.

If you are someone who experiences low self-esteem, at least at times, it will help you to see how your ability to use willpower can be affected. It also helps to understand why criticising others for their lack of willpower is so unhelpful. It does nothing but highlight their own guilt and self-criticism, lowering their self-esteem even more and making matters worse as a result. They become even less likely to change their ways and more likely to try to defend themselves, usually with some form of denial such as refusing to acknowledge that there's any problem.

Low self-esteem undermines willpower, and understanding this connection is a crucial key. There are two main obstacles to using willpower for those with low self-esteem:

Peer Pressure

One place to notice the effect low self-esteem has on your willpower is in how much you are influenced by the people around you. I'm describing this as peer pressure because this is how it's often understood, but it's far more prevalent and problematic than the cliché of the group of kids sneaking cigarettes behind the bicycle sheds.

There is the example of the expectations of a family in conflict with an individual's own agenda for his or her life. There's the cultural encouragement to spend and consume over a personal desire to save or get out of debt. There's the pressure on so many teenagers to be skinny, do drugs and/or have sex, when each of these can so often have disastrous effects on their lives.

More specific examples could include the woman who wants to stop eating between meals, but her colleagues keep bringing in cakes to share at the office; a smoker with chronic bronchitis who wants to quit but spends his social time at a pub where all his friends smoke; a teenager who wants to save money, while all her friends have the latest design of mobile phone; a woman who would prefer to order a salad in a restaurant, but her friends are ordering pizza; a man who feels he's had enough to drink, but the group he's with are ordering another round.

What all these examples have in common is a conflict between individual willpower and the collective will of a group. The group may be a circle of friends, a family or, in a wider sense, our culture. This can be very much a part of everyday life, and you may be able to find a wide variety of examples of your own. The question is, do you go with the crowd or do what you want to do? If you go with the group *every time*, you can, perhaps without even realising what you're doing, undermine the power of your individual will.

Those with lower self-esteem will tend to go with the group more often. They will tend to be more influenced by fashion, brand names, marketing and advertising. They may be more swayed by celebrities, by other people's opinions in general, and less inclined to rely on their own thinking.

Low self-esteem means there can be quite a strong mistrust of your own ability to make decisions that are right for you. Any sense of self-worth tends to be gained through the approval of others, so the opinions of the group are going to win every time. Low self-esteem means that what matters most is what the group wants, how the group behaves, what the group thinks and what the group believes.

This isn't necessarily a completely bad thing and it is always a matter of degree. We are social animals, we live in groups and communities, and a real sense of belonging is a crucial element in our lives. Being part of a group makes a huge contribution to our health and emotional well-being. It is a wonderful way to live, and part of that is to conform to that group, to identify yourself with it and to experience the powerful support that comes from a real sense of belonging. Much can be achieved by individuals who are supported in this way.

It becomes a problem, though, when your own willpower is blocked because approval from the group is always more important to you than your own personal needs and goals. The group isn't necessarily always right, and most of all it isn't necessarily right about what's good for you to do.

This is about being *too* concerned with what others think, whether it's about the shape of your body, what you eat, what clothes you wear, what career you follow, how you spend your time or your money, what car you drive or what your living room looks like. If you're going to conform at all costs, your own willpower is redundant.

Your willpower gets blocked by your fear of stepping outside the group agreement. The risk of disapproval and rejection is a very powerful force in us all. It's the negative side of belonging to a group – *any* group. As soon as a group forms – whether it be your immediate family, a circle of friends, a department in a university or business, or even a more general sense of group such as 'middle-class teenagers' – certain views become accepted and left unchallenged because to challenge them is to risk alienation. Often unspoken and unnoticed, beliefs held by the group may seem so real that nobody would even think of questioning them. A particular group may even identify itself with rebellion, while strictly conforming to its own rules and regulations! Punks and Hell's Angels come to mind as examples of rebellious groups with fairly rigid ideas of how to behave and what to look like.

Nowhere is the combination of low self-esteem and peer pressure so disastrous than when it comes to using willpower with food. The overwhelming pressure in our culture to be slim has made this the overriding preoccupation, even obsession, of a great many of us. Of course it's a good idea to lose weight, assuming you are in fact overweight to begin with. But the prevailing significance of appearance does nothing to support genuine self-esteem – and in fact undermines it. This has major implications for using willpower with food.

Those with low self-esteem tend to see their problem entirely in terms of their size and shape, so that losing weight is the only reason they would want to use willpower with food. At the same time, a low sense of self-worth means they may care considerably less about nutrition. Weight loss is the major theme in their lives because they have taken on the ideal of 'being slim' as their own mission in life – *whether or not they achieve it.*

The wonderful paradox is that when people make the shift in motivation and start to eat in a way that reflects and enhances their self-worth, they do lose weight and they keep it off. They end up looking better, and there's nothing wrong with that, but the weight loss is a bonus while the real prize is stronger self-esteem.

Again, this is a matter of balance, a matter of degree. It's a good thing for overweight people to lose weight, but I always

encourage people who attend my courses to pay close attention to other benefits which come from using willpower with
food. These benefits (in their words) include: freedom, control,
empowerment, happiness, slowing down of the ageing process,
more tolerance, peace of mind, balance, no mood swings,
energy, feeling more relaxed, integrity, no more migraines,
more time, more money, strength of character, greater awareness, a feeling of being unburdened, vitality, better health,
improved sleep, less guilt, better digestion, improved immune
system. Sounds good, doesn't it?

This is where genuine self-esteem truly lies. And all too
often this is forgotten, ignored and discounted – simply because
all that matters is 'looking good'. Most people are so focused on
losing weight they completely discredit any other kind of motivation. When people aren't working towards building their
true *self-esteem*, they aren't working towards building their
willpower. This is why it doesn't work to try to develop willpower with food *solely to change the shape of your body*.

It's well known that low self-esteem plays a major role in
more extreme eating disorders such as anorexia and bulimia.[1]
It's perhaps less well known that these more severe problems
are at the extreme end of a spectrum, and that the same issues
are involved in a wide variety of unhappy relationships with
food that would never be described as disorders.

Simply understand that there's a big difference between

using willpower with food purely to improve your appearance and using it because you care about your health. The difference is self-esteem.

Self-punishment

One of the most common theories is that people turn to addictions to comfort themselves and in doing so ease or avoid difficult emotions. They feel miserable, so they distract themselves with food, drink, cigarettes or whatever, to suppress the unpleasant feelings.

These emotions may be sadness, disappointment, frustration or anger, as just a few examples.[2] They may be associated with unsatisfactory circumstances in life and unhappy relationships, either from the past or in the present. Many books and articles have been written that deal with this, with the promise that when those feelings and issues are faced, the addiction fades as a result.

We'll look at this more in another chapter, but as far as self-esteem is concerned, it's important to see that when addiction is associated with low moods, it's really self-esteem that's the crucial issue. Of course, people don't only turn to addictive behaviour when they feel down; addictions are often part of everyday life, good times, intimacy and even celebration. But as far as 'negative' emotions are concerned, *your mood will drop whenever your self-esteem drops*. At those times when you are feeling despondent, unmotivated, depressed or just plain miserable, it can be extremely helpful to understand it as an experience of lower self-esteem. This may have its roots in your past but it's your present judgement of yourself that creates the real misery, your judgement that you are unworthy or incompetent and you don't deserve what you have or what you want. It may well be that you don't want to have the bad feelings, but lower self-esteem means that, far from wanting to nurture and take care of yourself, you're more likely to want to punish yourself.

On the other hand, it's entirely possible to have high esteem and respect for yourself and to feel difficult emotions at the same time. Maybe you feel angry about something somebody said to you, or you feel frustrated that things aren't going how you want or sad about something you've lost. You can still have a strong sense of your own worth in the middle of all this, even though you may feel genuinely miserable. Often, it's not the difficult feelings that undermine willpower it's the low self-esteem.

It's helpful to remember that the lower moods are connected to lower self-esteem. There may well be something that happened or didn't happen in your life to trigger this off but it's an important step to acknowledge *your own criticism of yourself* as part of the package. It's the low self-esteem that makes the feelings so problematic and so persistent. There's nothing so depressing as believing you're worthless and totally incompetent. Who wouldn't be depressed at that? Maybe you never get that down on yourself, but even if you fall into this just a bit, every now and then, it makes a big difference if you can name what's going on. When you own your part in generating these emotions, you get to see that you have a part in overcoming them. It may take effort and persistence, but this is a problem that you can do something about.

Stronger Self-Esteem

The crucial question is, how will you seek to regain your self-esteem at those times when it has faltered?[3] Your familiar strategies may well be addictive behaviours: retail therapy, drugs, a binge or whatever it is that does it for you. At best, though, they temporarily blot out the pain of lower self-esteem. They don't restore your esteem – and I bet you know that! In fact, quite the reverse is true. Turning to your addiction lowers your self-esteem even more because you then beat yourself up for not having any willpower! And so the cycle continues.

The truth is that your self-esteem will rise and fall all through your life, whether you are aware of this or not. It's also true that it is possible to learn how to develop higher self-esteem in general. You will find many directions towards building and maintaining stronger self-esteem as you go through this book, especially in the Step by Step section for this chapter. When you see the connection between self-esteem and willpower, you will be able to see the way forward.

In order to do this, we need to understand that two things work together to generate strong, healthy self-esteem. These are a sense of worth combined with a sense of competence. A sense of worth means knowing that no matter what you do, you can always find love for yourself, you can be on your own side and see value in your life. Acknowledging your worth as a human being is crucial, whether or not you are applying an ounce of willpower. It provides you with the motivation to start and the optimism to continue. If this looks like a very tall order for you, it will be important for you to look for guidance on this aspect of self-esteem. Some people find this guidance in books and courses on self-esteem while others access this quality of self-acceptance through various spiritual or religious disciplines.

The second factor that builds self-esteem is a sense of competence, and this is much more relevant to our topic of willpower. A sense of competence relates to how confident you are that you can cope (more or less) with life in general. This means that any time you start to use your will more powerfully, you'll be enhancing your self-esteem because you'll be building your sense of competence in life. You'll be demonstrating to yourself that you can do what you set out to do.[4]

So, stronger self-esteem supports willpower. And developing willpower enhances your self-esteem. There's a cyclical cause-and-effect relationship between the two. There's nothing like using willpower to take control of addiction to develop a stronger sense of competence. And there's nothing like it to confirm to yourself that you matter, that you are worth taking care of.

This is something that only you can do; you cannot look for it from someone else. You need to find it within you and act on it in the real world. That's where willpower comes in. And that's what's at stake.

This means using willpower in spite of all that's stacked against you. It means using willpower even though you don't expect to succeed, even though you don't think you're worth it, even though you'll be strongly tempted to cave in halfway through. It means going ahead and doing it anyway, acting as if you believe you can do it.

Don't wait for higher self-esteem. Look at what we've covered in this chapter and understand that it all needs to be taken into consideration. Realise that success with willpower may not feel like 'you' and may not be something you feel comfortable with at first. See using willpower as one extremely powerful way to develop stronger self-esteem. Make that your conscious aim and using willpower will bring you such life-enhancing rewards you'll want to continue.

Apathy or Joy

No matter what it is that you exercise your willpower over –
overeating, shopping, time in front of the TV – every result you
achieve can be a way for you to affirm your sense of ability and
worth. This cause-and-effect cycle doesn't end here, though,
because, in turn, any enhancement in self-esteem has the
knock-on effect of strengthening your willpower.

What makes the difference is to make these changes with
self-esteem in mind. Ask yourself if you are acting to conform
with others' expectations of you, or from some vague sense
that you 'should' or 'ought to do' something about this. Are
you wanting to make changes in order to impress others, and
are you caught up in values and goals that are not really your
own? Or are you using willpower because you've decided that
you matter?

When, by using willpower, you call into question the values
and behaviour of your peer group, you are taking a very brave
step. You risk some level of rejection or disapproval, no matter
how subtle, no matter how friendly and well intended it is. But
this risk is essential if you are to develop strong trust and a
high regard for yourself. Taking the risk of using your own
will, even when it doesn't conform with the group, rewards
you with higher self-esteem.

If popularity is what you're after, don't go for it at the
expense of your self-esteem. In the long run, strong self-esteem

is not only attractive but essential to healthy and mutually supportive relationships of all kinds. The more respect you have for yourself, the more likely you are to receive it from others. The more you have a real belief in your own abilities and your own worth, the more likely others will come to appreciate the same qualities in you.

Many people don't realise that their level of self-esteem is in their own hands. And they are so used to having low self-esteem they think it's just how they are, having no clue as to what a difference higher self-esteem could make to their lives.

Trying to develop willpower without developing self-esteem is tough. This is why I said that willpower and self-esteem go hand in hand. It's difficult, maybe even impossible, to sustain one for any length of time without the other.

Stronger self-esteem turns using willpower from an insurmountable burden into an exciting adventure. It doesn't mean being perfect. Good self-esteem is not arrogance, vanity or pride in false characteristics or empty achievements. It simply means being your own best friend, and it's completely natural for us to prefer it. As we saw at the beginning of this chapter, most of us would rather be our own best friend than our own worst enemy.

Strong self-esteem doesn't happen overnight. Gaining and restoring self-esteem is an on-going process, and using willpower is an essential part of that process. It's unlikely to be plain sailing but I can't think of anything more worthwhile. The power of will and the power of self-esteem open up endless possibilities and can't fail to enhance your life. Even if you only take a few steps, ever so gradually, it will begin to make the crucial difference between hopelessness and possibility, between apathy and joyful creativity. What more could you want out of life?

Step by Step

★ **Learn to identify self-esteem and how it shows up in your life** – For example, low self-esteem can show up as having little motivation to do anything at all, let alone anything challenging and life-changing. Most of us go through periods of time when we are indecisive and lazy. We might complain about things, either to ourselves or others, but do very little to change them. But is this a temporary phase or is it taking over your life? It's important to recognise such phases as an aspect of low self-esteem, because then you can track the source and start to do something about it.

★ **Observe how and why your self-esteem rises and falls** – Notice if your willpower becomes stronger or fades in tune with your self-esteem.

★ **Notice that using willpower strengthens your self-esteem** – Know that by using willpower – to take control of addiction, to delay gratification, to face a fear, to control impulses

– you have a powerful route to restoring your self-esteem. Pay attention to this because it provides you with motivation for your future use of willpower. An improvement in self-esteem may be subtle and may not be immediate, but any *experience* you have is precious – and infinitely more powerful than reading about it in a book.

★ **Get a perspective on how much self-esteem you have** – by comparing how you treat yourself with how you treat others. If you look at all those ways in which you don't take care of yourself, would you wish that on those you love? Would you treat them that way or want them to behave in that way?

★ **Identify all your positive motivation** – If you learn how to use your willpower, in what ways will you benefit? Motivation could be experienced as a threat (if I don't stop smoking, I'll die) or as a reward (if I stop smoking, I'll feel liberated). It's likely you have a mixture of both these types of motivation, but as much as possible, focus on rewards you hope to gain, including higher self-esteem. Negative threats tend to increase guilt and self-criticism, so it's best to keep them to a minimum.

★ **Identify your personal motivation** – Are you setting out to accomplish things purely for yourself or to fulfil other people's expectations of how you should be? There may be elements of both; what's important is a healthy balance.

Make sure you have a strong element of selfishness in your use of willpower, and be clear about how *your* life will be better as a result.

★ **Act 'as if'** – Whenever you need to make any decisions, it's a good idea to ask yourself what you would do in this situation if you had higher self-esteem. In this way you can find an answer that's more consistent with higher self-esteem – which in turn helps to create it.

★ **Identify stepping stones** – Perhaps you're reading this book with one particular problem area in mind, such as smoking or overeating. That's fine, and it's fine to focus your attention on this one achievement, but it can be helpful to look at other possibilities as well and to see them as part of the process. Exercising the power of your will in any one area will reward you with even a small sense of accomplishment. This provides you with a knock-on effect on another…and another… The stepping stones might be clearly related to your main goal, but not necessarily. Tidying up your bedroom could be a stepping stone the day before a job interview. Does that sound weird? Just try it, or something similar, and notice what you get out of it.

★ **Notice if you are wanting to use willpower in a competitive way** – Are you in a competition, either with specific people in your life or with other people in general? Do you want to use willpower to look better, prove your worth or appear superior? None of this supports genuine self-esteem.

★ **Keep your achievements to yourself** – in order to develop your own, internal sense of esteem and what it means to you to exercise the power of your own will. Of course this will partly depend on what you are wanting to use your willpower for, but especially when it comes to quitting smoking or taking control of overeating, it's good not to tell anyone what you're up to. If you haven't done this before, if you're the sort of person who tells everyone everything, try keeping it a secret and see what a difference it makes. If you don't like keeping things private, you can always go back to your old ways. Often people talk about their accomplishments ('Look at me, I've stopped smoking!' or 'Look at me, I've lost weight!') to try to gain some sense of achievement. Perhaps a response ('Well done!') seems to provide it, but you may well find it has a hollow ring to it. Admiration from others is always temporary and often it's *never enough*. This is the real killer to the motivation to continue with your challenge, or set a new one, and undermines your next battle with will. What's the point when nobody really cares? And even if they do – *so what*? By keeping it all to yourself, you stay focused on your own personal and private self-esteem. After all, self-esteem is the esteem *you* have for *yourself*. Which brings us to our next point.

★ **Be your own fan club** – Acknowledge your achievements by developing the habit of self-congratulation. This builds your willpower because it both rewards you for what you've done and motivates you towards your next achievement. This is a private process; it doesn't belong to anybody else. Begin to take moments throughout every day when you simply call to mind what you have achieved. Watch out for thinking you didn't do enough, or do something well enough; let that thought pass and return to what you *did* do. Then conduct a mini-celebration of yourself in your head, for just a few moments. Many people are taught as children that a feeling of pride is a bad thing, and if this is the case for you, this could represent your biggest breakthrough. I'm not talking about bragging to people about how great you are. In fact, the whole world could think you're totally fabulous, but if you don't think so yourself you will suffer. You'll be at odds with external success – compliments, awards, money – if you don't believe you deserve them. Then, some form of self-sabotage is almost inevitable.

★ **Be as courageous as you can** – Higher self-esteem can be frightening and it's worth pointing out that this fear can keep you stuck in chronic low self-esteem. There's something safe about being someone who is fundamentally incapable of any real or lasting change. You don't expect anything more of yourself, and anyway, you don't deserve

anything better. People who resign themselves to medioc-
rity and who think as small as they can are sure to succeed!
If you suspect that you've already given up on yourself too
much and for too long, just know that this is always a decision that can be reversed.

★ **Take special care with willpower if you have anorexic
tendencies** – Willpower, like anything in life, can be abused.
Too much air, water or sleep can be just as bad for us as
too little, and can even kill. If you prioritise your health
and genuine self-esteem, you will be able to tell when you
are using too much willpower with food. Anorexia arises
from poor self-esteem, which means low interest in health
and way too much interest in other people's opinions about
appearance.

Where There's a Will: Sarah

I did Gillian's course on overeating because I wanted to lose
weight. I wanted to lose two stone and I wanted to keep it off,
which I have never managed to do since my early teens. It
seemed to me that I was completely incapable of doing this,
even though I wanted it very much. I'm a wife, a mother to a
beautiful three-year-old girl, a mature student and a part-time
administrator. I cope with all this and I really know I can do
anything I want, but I would fall apart when it came to food.

What is helping is to realise that the missing link for me was self-esteem. Anyone looking at my life from the outside would probably think I had good self-esteem but I did not. It didn't make any difference what I achieved, and I know I have done quite well. I think this is because I come from a family of high achievers and I have ended up very much following in their footsteps. My mother in particular, as I'm taking very much the same path as her in life. I think I took on her tendency to use self-criticism to drive herself to achieve more, but whatever I do, it's never enough.

What helps me now is to remember that my achievements don't stop my self-criticism. What stops the self-criticism is unconditional self-acceptance. And unconditional means not conditional on any achievements! So it's not about when I lose the weight, then I'll be happy and then I'll esteem myself. I'm still a long way from accepting myself unconditionally, but I certainly am beginning to see improvements.

Mostly I still want to lose weight, but what I realise is that I can be more compassionate with myself along the way. I feel much less guilty about eating even when I do eat the wrong things, and I'm doing a lot less of that. I never used to think about what was healthy, only whether or not I wanted to eat something and whether or not it would make me fat. I eat in a much more healthy way now and I actually want to do that. I am losing weight and I'm pleased about that, but I think about food in a completely different way now and I feel much less desperate about the weight. I think that's made a big difference. It seems that the less desperate I become, the more it's happening.

In general, I think less about doing everything to please other people and quite a bit more about doing what's right for me. This has been a very big step for me. I feel a lot more relaxed now. I've become less of the entertainer of the family and this is working better for all three of us.

Notes

1. 'Strong associations for eating disorders were found with low self-esteem.' From a study of 2,862 girls between 12 and 21 years of age, reported in the *International Journal of Eating Disorders* (31:261–273, 2002).

2. Something else to take into consideration is that it is not a good idea to suppress emotions. Neuroscientist Candace Pert, PhD, speaks of this in her book *Molecules of Emotion* (Simon & Schuster, 1997): '…the chronic suppression of emotions results in a massive disturbance of the psychosomatic network… I believe *all* emotions are healthy, because emotions are what unite mind and body. Anger, fear, sadness, the so-called negative emotions, are as healthy as peace, courage, and joy. To repress these emotions and not let them flow freely is to set up a dis-integrity in the system, causing it to act at cross-purposes rather than as a unified whole.'

3. Nathaniel Branden, PhD, the leading authority on self-esteem, suggests that six factors play the vital role: living consciously, self-acceptance, self-responsibility, self-assertiveness, living purposefully and personal integrity. He describes them in his book *The Six Pillars of Self-Esteem* (Bantam, 1994).

4. Nathaniel Branden makes this crucial point: 'It is not that achievements "prove" our worth, but rather that the process of achieving is the means by which we develop our effectiveness, our competence at living.'

CHAPTER THREE

From Slavery to Mastery

Mastering the skill of making choices

I wonder if you have any mixed feelings about willpower? Many people aren't convinced it's such a great thing because, although willpower is the only way to get the results they're after, using it means not being able to indulge any more. This is the love–hate relationship of addiction; you love to do it, you feel deprived if you don't – *and* it's making your life a misery. What a trap!

In this chapter I'm going to show you how to get out of this trap. In fact, it's essential to get out because you are unlikely to continue to use willpower if you feel like you're missing out on something, denying yourself or restricting yourself in some way.

This is an almost universal stumbling block to accessing willpower. People go on diets desperate to lose weight, but when they do they can't stop thinking about all the gooey treats they're not having. Smokers wish they had never started, but when they quit they find themselves pining for a puff, envious of others smoking, deprived and resentful about not being able to join in the fun.

The way out of this trap is a concept that's as simple and straightforward as it is profound: it's all about choice.[1] Of all the concepts we will look at, none is more central to willpower than choice. Willpower is the powerful use of your will, your will is free will and so willpower is all about making powerful free choices. A great many people try to use willpower without fully believing they are making a choice. If you do this you will run into big trouble.

If you haven't got a choice it's as if you're a slave. Slaves have precious little freedom at all. Slaves are forced to work, told where to go, what to do and when to do it. As a slave, your entire life is ruled and restricted by your master. In complete contrast, the master is someone who is totally free and in control of their entire universe.

In terms of willpower we could describe ourselves as either slaves or masters. It's really a matter of degree, from one extreme to the other, either more towards slavedom or more towards being the one who's in charge of it all. Of course, neither one of these extremes is likely to describe you, but I hope you can see – or start to think about if you haven't done so before – how the varying degrees of these two states mix together to influence your actions and your feelings in various areas of your life.

To take real-life examples, I would think that most adults believe they are in charge of what time they go to bed. If they're feeling a bit tired one evening, they might decide to turn in earlier than usual. Another evening, perhaps, they want to watch a TV show and so they stay up later. They have little or no conflict about it once they've decided what they want to do. But that same person could feel much more slave-like when it comes to food, quite unable to control the amounts they eat, as if some unseen power had them in their grips. Even when they try to diet they feel restricted and punished, so they don't keep it up for long.

Someone could have a great sense of mastery at work but feel and act more slave-like at home around their parents or partner. For others, it's as if they are slaves at work but masters in their own homes. Someone could feel very in control of their finances but a slave to nicotine.

Inasmuch as you are seeking more willpower in at least one area of your life, one way to understand much of the difficulty you have – and in doing so come closer to a solution – is to see that you are acting and feeling more slave-like in this regard and not as masterful as you could be. After all, if you were the master in this circumstance, you would be completely in charge of whatever you wanted to do and there would be absolutely no question or difficulty about carrying it out.

The reason I'm describing this in these terms is to show you that a major part of your ability to make the changes you want lies in shifting the balance. One big key to using willpower – possibly the biggest key – is in simply moving away from slavedom towards mastery. The big question is how you do this. How did you become a slave in this area, where willpower doesn't work and never will? And, more importantly, how do you get out of it?

The answer lies in the ownership of choice. Slaves have few choices. Masters have all the choices. It's not hard to see who is going to have the most powerful free will. When you own your choices you, too, gain mastery of your own will.

Owning Your Choices

★ **Know that you have got choices** – Sometimes you hear people say that something was 'not an option'. It's an expression that's often used but it's almost never true. You could be stuck between the devil and the deep blue sea, but you still have choices: the devil or the sea. Difficult choices are still choices. Bad choices are still choices. No matter how stuck in a particular situation you seem to be, there are always alternatives. Maybe if you look closer, and in a more honest way, there is an option you're not considering because it's not ideal. It's not the perfect solution, it's not how you really want it to be, so you've decided it's not an option at all. This denial of having any choice at all keeps you stuck in slavery, undermining your willpower.

★ **Know what your choices are between** – Be as honest as possible with yourself about the whole picture of what it is you're choosing. As much as you can, because you may not know exactly what some of the consequences will be. One of the choices you have is not to make any changes at all. This can be tough if you feel the pressure of illness, excess weight or other consequences that seem to be forcing you to make changes. When you accept the truth of your essential freedom, through, you take a step towards mastering how to make the choices you really want to make.

★ **Know that you are the one who's going to be making those choices and nobody else** – It could be that you want something done for you. Or maybe you want a magic, instant 'cure' so that you don't need to put any effort into it. When you let go of those unrealistic expectations, when you see that willpower is completely up to you and your own effort and it will always be, you'll be able to see your way through.

★ **Know that you can only choose for the present time** – It's impossible to make one choice to use willpower that will last into the future. All you can do is choose for now and be willing to see what happens as you go along. If you try to make a long-term commitment you'll feel deprived, as if you didn't have the freedom to change your mind.

★ **Remember the four points above at those times when you want to use willpower** – It's not just a matter of understanding the idea of it while you're reading this book. The only thing that's going to make a real difference is to connect with these concepts so that you can access the power of your will. This takes effort and deliberate intention at first, but after a while it becomes your natural way of thinking.

When it comes to taking control of addiction, the worst thing you can do is to try to use willpower without first taking these steps to own choice. What you've got then is a slave assuming they're free. Not only does this not work, it actually creates a great deal of struggle and upset, making willpower a bitter pill to swallow.

An attempt at self-control *without owning choice* is exactly what most people think willpower is – and this is exactly why so many people say they don't have any. They aren't even sure they want any in the first place because using it is such a miserable experience. When using willpower leaves you feeling deprived, what would otherwise be a dream come true – finally some control over your addiction – turns into a nightmare.

As a slave to your addiction, you need first of all to free yourself by owning your choices. Then, willpower happens as a natural state available to all masters. To do this, you simply stop telling yourself you have no choice or you have no options. You stop thinking in terms of forcing yourself and that you 'have to' or 'can't' do things. You understand that you won't really be using willpower until you first of all own choice. Then, you start to make free choices to direct the power of your will in the ways you truly want.

Let's look at this in more detail, because although the idea of choosing is dead simple, many people have developed fairly complicated ways of evading and denying it.

How to Be a Slave

Make a commitment

This is the same as saying that any time you quit, you don't have the freedom to return to the addictive behaviour. In other words, as soon as you start to use your willpower, you are committed to that course of action. Making a commitment is undoubtedly well intended but it creates problems because it denies free choice. When people get committed, they get locked up and they don't have freedom any more. That's the point of being committed. As soon as you make a commitment you're a slave again and you'll feel as if you no longer have freedom of choice.

Making a commitment undermines willpower to such an extent that people are likely to postpone it indefinitely. For example, those smokers who believe that quitting means they must make a commitment never to smoke again are the least likely to stop. The smoker who is most likely to stop – and who will have the least traumatic time in the process – is one who is willing to give it a go without making long-term predictions.

If you think you could never use willpower without making a commitment, you will see how to make truly free choices later on. The key is to get to a place where you're sure of which choice you want to make and you've become skilled at carrying it out, while knowing you're still a completely free agent.

Believe you don't have any willpower

This is the denial of a different choice – the choice to take control of addiction – and it usually comes from having failed many times in the past. If you're taking the trouble to read this book, it's very possible you have some experience behind you of failing with willpower. You may accept that you've got willpower in some areas of your life but none when it comes to this one issue. Or maybe you tell yourself you have no willpower at all in anything you do. Either way, it's another way to deny free choice.

The fact that you failed in the past is not a problem; the problem is the conclusion you've come to as a result. The conclusion is that no matter what you do, no matter how hard you try, you'll never succeed at this willpower challenge. Repeated failures lead people into a state called 'learned helplessness' so that they don't actually try to use willpower because they're already convinced it isn't going to work. It can even mean that you don't actually want to make any changes, so you don't try to use willpower because you don't feel in the least bit inspired to do so.

Learned helplessness has been researched quite a bit in a number of scientifically controlled experiments. It is well established that human beings and animals alike, when confronted with a problem to which there is no solution, will at some point give up trying. Subjects are given simple problems with what seem to be simple solutions. But the problems are rigged, and no matter what they do and no matter how hard they try, they are impossible to solve. At some point learned helplessness sets in and they stop trying. Then – even when the situation is changed and a solution does become possible – *attempts to solve the problems are no longer made*.

This might seem so obvious you wonder why experiments are needed to demonstrate it! The important point is that the learned helplessness persists even when a solution becomes possible. I cannot emphasise enough how relevant this could be to your success with willpower. By the time you get to the end of this book, you will have the solution to a problem with any addictive behaviour, and it's a solution you may not have had access to before. However, you could be in danger of not even seeing it if you hold on to your belief that you don't possess willpower. Your learned helplessness could create failure before you've made any attempt at all, leading you to make only feeble, token efforts at best. It also undermines your motivation to change, so that although your life will improve significantly through using willpower, it's tough for you to fully grasp that possibility.

It will be important for you to know that you don't need to believe you'll succeed in order to succeed. Simply be willing to try by considering the possibility of success this time. You will, however, need to use what you learn in this book. If you repeat the same strategies you've used before you're likely to get the same results! More failure. More learned helplessness. Stronger belief that you don't have willpower. Undermined self-esteem. You need to try something different – but before that, you need to be willing to try.

One survey reported that an astounding 83 per cent of smokers wish they had never started in the first place.[2] However, learned helplessness means that most of them aren't putting time and effort into quitting. They've learned to expect failure, and explain this to themselves by saying they don't have any willpower. The picture is much the same for those who are overweight and have a long history of failure at dieting.

Judge yourself harshly for the choices you make

Many people resist owning choice because they think that if it's their choice, it's also their fault. If you tend to beat yourself up a lot for choices you've made, denying choice is an attractive solution. You've no doubt heard youngsters claim, 'It wasn't me, I didn't do it!' in order to escape some blame and maybe some punishment. A similar scenario can get acted out inside your own head.

If it's not your fault, someone or something else is going to get the blame. In which case, you'll have a good explanation for your addiction that is quite beyond your control. It might be your parents' fault, your genes or some other circumstance in your life, either past or present, that you can do nothing about.

Avoiding excessive blame and judgement is part of the reason why addiction is often explained as a physical disease. Unfortunately, it's become one of the most popular ways to evade personal choice: 'It's not my fault – it's a biochemical, inherited, genetic, social disease and I just can't help it!' Perhaps some version of this means you stop being so hard on yourself but it also means you're helpless to do anything about it. Willpower disappears again.

Owning choice means owning your decision. Work towards becoming more forgiving of yourself (the self-worth side of self-esteem) and you'll be more likely to acknowledge free choice *even when you make choices you later regret*. Then, you can start to create what you really want in your life because you own your responsibility for it. After all, if you're not responsible for something, you can do very little about it.

Have no trust in yourself

Maybe you fear that if you tell yourself you have the freedom to indulge, you will. So you try to cope with this fear of failure by denying freedom of choice. You try to keep yourself in check by pretending you have no alternative.

Notice if your thoughts around using willpower start with: I mustn't…I shouldn't…I have to…I can't…I've got to…I ought to…I'm not able to… This way of thinking denies your choices, turning self-control into self-denial. This way of thinking doesn't work – especially in the long term.

When you begin to question this thinking, your fear of failure may surface and create some resistance. Remember how to own choice and start to make the choices you really do want to live with. In time, your fear of failure will fade as you begin to trust yourself more to make the choices that you really do want to live with.

Why Slavery Doesn't Work
Rebellion

The drive to be free is found almost everywhere in life. Trap an animal and it will immediately seek an escape, because to be trapped is to be extremely vulnerable. Being trapped is dangerous, survival is at stake, so it's no mystery why escape is the number one priority.

An example of rebellion in action could be found in the resistance you may have experienced to reading this book. In some way, perhaps, you think I will tell you that you must take control and change your ways. You might have assumed you'll be told to make one choice over another and, worst of all, that this choice must last for ever. I would say this is a pretty good reason to put this book down and not to pick it up again!

Of course this rebellious reaction is about far more than just reading this book; it's about whatever it is you want to use your willpower for. On the one hand you want to take control of your addiction, but on the other it seems that if you do your freedom to do it will be gone – not surprising then that you find it tough to use willpower.

Curiously, rebellious people are sometimes described as being strong-willed, but at least as far as addiction is concerned they are not exercising will at all. They are told they can't or mustn't do something – and so they are compelled to do it! This is an automatic, knee-jerk reaction, and there's not a great deal of choice in that.

We can easily see the effects of rebellion in whole societies where efforts have been made to eliminate illegal drugs. In the United States, for example, making alcohol illegal during

Prohibition caused a sharp increase in its use. It is now becoming more widely known that forbidding food means we'll eat more of it. No matter how it's put across, the message that 'you have to stop doing this' simply doesn't work.

Pay attention to any signs of rebelliousness you experience. Remember that before you can rebel, there has to be a rule or a restriction of some kind. Throw out the rules. Question your self-imposed restrictions. Remember you have free choices about what you do and you'll see that there's nothing to rebel against.

More intense and persistent cravings

Intense and overwhelming feelings of desire and compulsion are created when we deny our freedom to choose. If we deny choice we feel trapped and this means we need to get free. With this logic, getting free means returning to the addiction, which is why we crave it more and refuse to let it fade, naturally, out of our lives.

I met a woman recently who told me she had quit smoking twenty years ago and still craved a cigarette every day, especially in the evenings. She said, and these were her words, that she felt deprived because she wasn't able to smoke a cigarette. This is what I would call a persistent craving. It's caused by her denial of choice – what she thinks she can't have, she wants all the more – and it's completely unnecessary and avoidable.

Low moods and feelings of deprivation[3]

I had been feeling quite irritable for a couple of days after I stopped smoking, when my counsellor pointed out to me (one more time!) that I had complete freedom to return to smoking. In an 'Aha!' moment it suddenly clicked, the irritability disappeared instantly and never returned. That's when I knew I really had hold of something important because I experienced it myself. If you don't experience this yourself – and it's possible you haven't yet – this chapter simply won't have the same impact. This experience is when you know you've got the freedom to take action – smoking or overeating for example – while not actually doing it.

Once you know that it's denial of free choice that causes the low moods associated with using willpower – irritability, loss, deprivation, self-pity, frustration, sadness – then you can do something about them. Often the moods are projected on to other issues – career prospects, relationships, money problems – so that the problem seems to be 'out there'. Or sometimes these low moods are ascribed to unbalanced body chemistry, which is something we'll explore later.

You can only gain this essential experience of what I'm describing *after* you've taken control of addiction. Once you've grasped that you've got the freedom to relapse *even though you're not doing so*, you'll find that the feelings of deprivation and the low moods evaporate.

Stress

A great deal of research has linked having no freedom of choice with stress.[4] It is said, for example, that one of our greatest sources of stress is being stuck in a traffic jam. Why is sitting in a comfortable chair, listening to your favourite music on the radio, so stressful? Mostly because you have absolutely no choice about it.

The link between choice and stress is quite simple to demonstrate in experiments, with both animal and human subjects. You give two groups something potentially stressful, such as a loud, irritating noise. Both groups experience exactly the same amounts and levels of noise, but one group has the freedom to turn the noise off while the other hasn't. When physical symptoms are measured, the group who had a choice are far less stressed. Even if their efforts didn't in fact reduce the noise at all, simply their belief that they could do something about their problem made the difference.

This finding was confirmed by a massive study of office workers in England known as the Whitehall study. Researchers tracked over 10,000 civil servants for five years, looking in particular at what contributed to the everyday stress they encountered in the workplace. The stress they measured showed up years later in very real symptoms of heart disease, such as angina.

They looked for the causes of stress in personal characteristics such as how competitive, miserable or aggressive they were. They looked at their workload and how much support they received. One factor alone emerged as the key to ongoing stress at work. This factor was individual control. What made all the difference to their daily stress was whether or not an individual had 'complete discretion and independence in determining how and when the work was to be done'. Those with a far greater sense of free choice about their work had significantly less stress and, as a result, less heart disease.

When people try to use willpower but have no sense of their own independence in determining how and when, stress is an inevitable consequence. As a result, it can seem to us that using willpower is stressful, so it's no wonder we stop using it. Once again, owning your personal choices is the solution.

Indecisiveness and procrastination

It seems obvious that the less you own your choices, the less likely that you'll be able to make them, so the more likely you are to be indecisive and put off taking action for as long as you possibly can. Good excuses for your procrastination will play an essential role!

Then, whenever you do set a goal and start to take some control over addiction, you could be doing nothing more than following orders from someone else. Following a diet is a good example of this, and sometimes smokers who attend a group to help them quit will go along with the group in a similar way.

You might have already noticed that this doesn't deliver the results you want in the long term. This is because you're not really using your willpower. Following orders means you're still a slave. You might gain some sense of security for a while but it's unlikely to last. If you're wondering why, see the section on rebellion, above.

Willpower Means Thinking

Owning choice doesn't necessarily mean you *do* anything different. It's a shift in thinking. When you have made this shift and connect with a genuine sense of choice, you will find that things start to change. You will feel different, much more positive, more in control, more motivated and infinitely more able to access your genuine willpower.

It will help you to know what you're up against. In general, our culture is fairly unaware of this issue around choice, so it's not at all surprising if it's new to you. I see examples of this all over the place, but just one example I read in a newspaper recently made me smile. The article was about the popularity of tennis in Australia, so much so that many people put tennis courts in their gardens even though there's no room for anything else. The journalist wrote: 'Mothers were often forced to hang the washing on the net.' The image that comes to my mind includes a SWAT team, complete with helicopters and semi-automatic rifles!

I've not been to Australia, but I suspect these mothers aren't really being forced at all. In fact, they have many choices. They could take their washing to a laundrette, they could buy dryers, or they could hang washing inside their houses. And if the garden is big enough for a tennis court it would be big enough for a washing line anyway.

My aim is not to change the way Australians do their laundry, it's to emphasise how much you'll need to pay attention to this issue of choice. It's going to require very deliberate effort to remember that you've got choices in a world where almost everyone forgets this fact. It is going to take some conscious attention on your part.

This is not a huge step – but it is an essential one. You are not going to be able to own choice without doing some very deliberate thinking. It requires you directing your thoughts. If you're not willing to do this, you'll get the same old stuff, which will probably be an 'Oh phooey!' reaction. You decide to cut out fried food, for example, but when you're faced with fried food later, you say 'Oh phooey! I'll start that diet tomorrow.' This is why you can fail with willpower even though you're very clear about what behaviour you wish to change and why.

Willpower doesn't happen while you're thinking about something else. In fact, the essential use of will is in your choice to think or not to think. Your first and most fundamental choice is to think one thing or to think another – or to go into a daze and not think about anything much at all. You've got the choice to evade thoughts by distracting yourself from them. And you also have the choice to focus your attention on a thought and hold it in your mind.

Making a choice to think is the way you access the power of your will. You deliberately consider what your choices are, what the consequences of different choices will be and what actions you will choose to take. At first it's laborious, but the more you practise, the easier it becomes.

Conscious attention is what makes the difference, because it's only then that you can think through your first, automatic response and consider another. But I'm not suggesting that you need to become 100 per cent attentive 100 per cent of the time. It's simply not possible to be completely aware of our world and our thoughts all the time, and to some extent functioning on automatic is part of our lives and always will be. We very much need to be on automatic sometimes in order to function.

A good example of this is found in driving, when we perform the motions of driving a car while our mind is on something else entirely, perhaps a relationship problem or some issue at work. When we first learn how to drive, it seems so complicated. There is so much to think about, to be aware of, and so much to do all at once. Clutch. Rearview mirror. Turn the wheel. Look where you're going. Take your foot off the brake. And you haven't even moved yet. We need to be conscious of it all and it's a lot to learn. As we practise, though, much of it becomes automatic and we drive for hours, hardly aware of what we're doing.

Addictive behaviour becomes automatic in the same way, as we repeat, learn and practise these habits. Our thinking around them becomes largely automatic and unconscious too, and that's when it seems our will is not our own. It seems things just happen, we end up smoking or overeating or whatever, and our own will was never a part of it. We need to get more conscious, more aware, before we can make the changes we want to make.

It's sometimes said that many people these days don't have particularly good powers of concentration, even for fairly short periods of time. This is partly because we have so many things to attend to in our lives and partly because some forms of our culture have encouraged this in us. Anyone who makes advertisements, TV shows, movies or music nowadays takes into account that their audience has about a three-second attention span. They aim to grasp your attention that fast, move to another image or message that fast and keep the pace going – or maybe you'll switch channels or switch off entirely. As a result, many of us don't have a very well-developed skill of focusing attention on any one thing for any longer than that. This makes it all the more likely that we'll 'switch off' as soon as there's a hint of anything that might be challenging, boring or uncomfortable.

Turning this around will take time and effort, but doesn't mean it's impossible. What I'm describing here is all about developing willpower – and it can never be done for you. You start to become aware of these automatic thoughts so that you can re-examine them. You question aspects and then replace some of them with new ways of thinking. In time, this new way of thinking becomes more automatic and more your natural way of thinking. When this happens people stop smoking, for example, and later on they wonder why and how they ever smoked so much. Not smoking has become the norm and it takes far less effort to continue with it. But initially, when they were first quitting, they needed to pay a lot of attention to using willpower.

If you are not willing to pay attention, what will happen is that you may decide on one course of action but later on go into automatic, losing sight of willpower and any sense of control at all. This is not because you changed your mind about what you wanted to accomplish, but because you didn't stay conscious when you needed to. You need to be conscious in those moments when you are attracted towards the addictive behaviour. You don't have a choice about that attraction but you do have a choice about what you do in response to it.

This is all about the addictive urge or craving, and the physical, chemical side to addiction. This is important because many people think they are controlled by the chemistry of a drug. This is the idea that you are dependent physically, that your biochemistry overrides your willpower so that the only alternative is the addictive drug – be it nicotine, sugar, chocolate, cocaine or anything else.

I've not discussed these widely held views yet because this is what we will deal with in the next few chapters. It's another issue of choice, though, because this theory says that the addictive substance chooses your actions, that you're a slave to or a victim of your own body chemistry. We will need to look carefully at this whole area so that we can see how to make choices to take control of addiction, and how to put those choices into action.

Part of this will include accepting that we can't have it all. We can free ourselves from slavery and gain more mastery of our universe – but we will never be in charge of absolutely everything. We do not become omnipotent, and so:

★ choosing to have one thing inevitably means not having something else;

★ some choices will not be available to us;

★ we can make mistakes and choose something we later regret.

Even so, we still have choices. The point is to work towards freely choosing how you really do want to live your life. For example, when you really accept that you're free to continue smoking for the rest of your life, you're more likely to get interested in quitting. And then by owning your choice you will be able to carry out quitting successfully, through knowing you're always free to return to smoking if that's what you choose.

There's tremendous value in remembering that you've got choices. First of all, using your willpower doesn't leave you feeling deprived. There'll undoubtedly be times when you feel *tempted*, but not at all *deprived*, because you know it's your own choice not to indulge. Secondly, you eliminate the powerful instinct to rebel, and that makes a big difference to long-term success. Thirdly, when free choice becomes a reality, the obsession and overwhelming cravings subside, along with guilt, anxiety and stress. And finally, it's only when you acknowledge your own choice in the matter that you can begin to let go of all those wonderful excuses. You just don't need them any more when you're free to choose whatever you want to do with your own life.

Owning choice doesn't always make it easy to use willpower, but it does make it easier, and most of all it makes it possible. Owning choice is the only effective way to access your willpower. It also strengthens your self-esteem.

Step by Step

★ **Practise choosing where you place your attention** – You could do this right now by deliberately switching your attention from this page to something else. You could bring your attention to yourself, thinking about how your body feels, both physically (is your chair soft or hard? how do your clothes feel on you?) and emotionally (sad, happy, calm, irritated?). Practise this several times a day, and if you want to, you could put up Post-it notes to remind you. In particular, practise switching attention from things outside you, including other people, to things inside you, including your thoughts and feelings. Deliberately switching your attention in this way is the key to willpower. Your willpower is inside you, and you need to look inside in order to access it.

★ **Start out by owning your choices, no matter what choices you're making** – If you continue addictive behaviour, start to choose it. Let yourself know that at least for now you are choosing the addiction – and that you can continue to do that for your whole life and never stop. Then, you begin with a sense of choice. Then, you can start to make the choices you really want to make. If you don't acknowledge choice first, you're still operating as if you're a captive slave with no will of your own.

★ **Make educated choices** – Tell the truth about what it is you're choosing, what's at stake, what the consequences of your actions will be. You own your choices fully by choosing the consequences along with the actions. For example, 'I choose to eat this tub of ice cream and feel nauseous and guilty afterwards' or 'I choose to smoke this cigarette and return to smoking all day, every day.' Remembering this when it counts will take deliberate effort.

★ **Whenever you lose sight of your motivation, remind yourself that you've got choices** – Remind yourself that you don't *have to* do anything, you don't *have to* change one thing about your life. You can continue exactly the way you are. When you honestly take that in, your motivation to make changes will appear. If you have any motivation at all, you'll know that you don't want to live this way. Put words to why that is, describing for yourself how your life might improve if you use your willpower in this area – and there's your motivation to change.

★ **Whenever you notice that you're procrastinating, remind yourself that you've got choices** – Trying to use willpower without owning choice is an extremely negative experience. While you deny your choices, the anxiety that comes from even thinking about using willpower will block you from getting started. Hence, procrastination. Start out by genuinely choosing to not change anything.

★ **Notice if you're waiting for someone or something else to do it for you** – Remember that owning choice is also about being willing to play your part in what you want to achieve – instead of merely reading this book passively, expecting magic. It's about being prepared to think about how this applies to you and what you want to achieve through this book. You could think of this book as a map – and a map is not the journey. The journey is the bit that only you can do. When you understand that nobody will ever come along and do this journey for you, you can start to take responsibility yourself.

★ **Own your choices about food, not your weight** – In terms of willpower, the choices that are open to you – and therefore the choices you can actually make – are choices about eating. When you start to make choices to eat less, one result is that you lose weight. It's very helpful to shift the focus of your choices on to the cause (eating more food than your body needs) instead of the effect (being overweight). When an overeater says, 'My goal is to lose two stone,' it's like a smoker saying, 'My goal is to lose this cough.' It misses the point.

★ **Become more aware of your choices** – with this powerful exercise. You'll need to get someone else involved in this, and they need to be the person or people you talk to the most. This could be people you work with, your partner, your best friends or your family. What you do is ask them to let you know every time they hear you say 'I have to…'

or 'I can't...' So, for example, if you say, 'I have to go to the shops now to buy a newspaper', they are going to remind you that you don't *have to* go. You have choices. Or perhaps you say, 'I can't make that phone call now because I want to watch TV.' It may be a good idea to watch the show and make the call later. The point is that you remember *you* are choosing what *you* do. This doesn't contradict advice from Chapter Two to keep things private, as long as you only use this exercise with regard to aspects of your life other than addictive behaviours. Developing a sense of choice in general will then be something you can more easily apply when it comes to willpower with addiction.

Where There's a Will: Nancy

I am a sixty-four-year-old retired schoolteacher, and most of my life has been spent either dieting or overeating. There seemed no middle road. Either I was eating what I 'should' or breaking free from that self-imposed censure and overeating until I was miserable.

The idea of having a choice has made a big difference. I had never realised before how negative and censorious I was about my eating. I was always telling myself I shouldn't, I can't, I must not – and then of course proceeding to eat what I wasn't supposed to, and feeling guilty, out of control and discouraged. Being aware that I always have a choice has freed me to decide, even in the midst of a binge, that I have a choice and do not have to continue eating.

In the past I could lose weight on a diet, but I could never keep the weight off, and I found that regaining the weight was humiliating and puzzling. How could I, who was in control of all the other areas of my life, be so obsessed and rebellious? There never seemed to be any psychological or personal problems bothering me; I just insisted on eating what I really wanted to, feeling guilty all the time, and damaging my self-esteem.

Now that I realise I always have a choice, I no longer think of food as the enemy. I no longer feel powerless and I can relax and enjoy eating. I not only have the choice of whether or not I am going to eat addictively, but I also have the choice to stop in the midst of overeating. When I choose to eat good food that nourishes my body, I also raise my self-esteem. When my motivation was to get thin it took a long time to see results, but when my motivation is good health and self-esteem I feel better right away. One day, even one meal, can make me feel in control and proud of myself. I then know I am living a healthier lifestyle, and the feeling of self-esteem enhances every area of my life.

My eating has changed dramatically. I certainly eat much less than I used to. The most dramatic change is when I'm actually overeating unthinkingly and then stop to give myself permission to keep eating as much as I want. That makes it possible for me to stop eating right then, and therefore I haven't binged at all since I went to the first class.

I remain very excited and pleased with my new way of eating. I am much more aware of when I want to eat addictively, and I have lots of good reasons for healthy eating. I'm finding that my choices are almost always made on the basis of what is really healthy, and I am able to stop at the end much more easily than I did at first. I feel much better physically and much better about myself.

Notes

1. There are people who believe that science has now proved that free will is nothing but an illusion. I see no need to argue with this theory because I live, as we all live, within the context of that illusion, where it at least *seems* that we have free choices about what actions we will and will not take. It seems to me, for example, that I can choose to wriggle my toes now – or not – and that this is in sharp contrast to my choosing whether or not you wriggle your toes now. The only reason free choice is ever called into question with the issue of willpower is not because of some complex debate on the nature of reality, but because of addictive desire. When it is said that people don't have free will with an addiction, what is meant is that they have no choice but to satisfy their craving. This book suggests an alternative and it's one that a great many people have used with success – whether or not they have read any of my books.

2. From the *British Medical Journal* (March 2002). The survey also found that smokers tended to hugely overestimate quitting in the future, with 53 per cent saying they expected to quit within the next two years, when in fact only 6 per cent quit over any two years.

3. 'Negative emotional states are especially likely in craving situations in which the drug in not available for use.' *Addiction* (96;1419–1432, 2001). This doesn't necessarily mean surrounding yourself with cigarettes or chocolate biscuits, although some people have found this to be a helpful strategy in gaining a real sense of freedom of choice. Mostly, what's needed is a change in attitude.

4. The Whitehall study is reported in the *Journal of Occupational Health Psychology* (3;402–409, 1998) and concludes: 'low job control, but not job demands, was found to predict new reports of coronary heart disease among London male and female civil servants.'

Stanford University neuroscientist and stress expert Dr Robert Sapolsky says, in his book *Why Zebras Don't Get Ulcers* (Freeman, 1994), that knowing you have a choice is 'an extraordinarily powerful variable in modulating the stress response'.

CHAPTER FOUR

Willpower on Prescription

The role of pharmaceuticals as aids to willpower

As you probably know, there is a wide range of pharmaceuticals available to assist your willpower in overcoming addiction. Nicotine Replacement Therapy (NRT) and the antidepressant bupropion (better known by the commercial name of Zyban) are offered as aids to quitting smoking. And a number of products work in different ways to help in taking control of overeating, including various kinds of appetite suppressants. In this chapter we look at where willpower sits alongside them.

As far as willpower is concerned, the message from pharmaceutical companies is not as clear as it could be. Advertisements for NRT, for example, say that you need to use your willpower as well as the product. They also say that your chances of success are doubled with NRT compared to using willpower alone. So willpower is essential – but only half as useful as nicotine replacement. As these figures are based on scientific evaluations, you could get the impression that willpower may not be so powerful after all.

You might wonder if the claims of ads really matter all that much to you and your willpower, but they matter because this issue is central to beating addiction. They matter because what this is really about is whether addiction is best tackled by altering your biochemistry or by altering the way you think. I expect that most people would say it's a combination of both. However, the extraordinary financial interests behind pharmaceuticals have contributed to a strong bias in our culture towards the biochemical solutions.

The pharmaceutical companies acknowledge the use of willpower but they don't seem to be completely sold on the idea of it. In the literature that accompanies the NRT products there's not a lot to explain what willpower is and no suggestions as to how you use it. The truth is that willpower – the power of the mind – doesn't fit very well into their view of things. Their view is that *addiction* means *physical dependency* and *chronic disease*, and many experts now assume that the problem is chemical and therefore the solution must be too.

The whole purpose of NRT is to deal with a physical dependency. The theory is that smokers have become physically dependent on nicotine and need to be weaned off it gradually, eventually recovering enough to function without it. No matter what product you use – gum, patches, inhalators, tabs, lozenges or nasal spray – NRT is designed to be used in a 'step-down' process, which simply means you use less and less as you go along. You use a weaker patch or you chew weaker-strength gum or you suck the lozenges less often, and the idea is that eventually your body and brain will have recovered, they won't need or crave nicotine any more and you will have successfully quit smoking.

NRT is the standard aid for smokers because it's been thoroughly researched and proven to work, but the vast majority of this extremely expensive research is funded by the pharmaceutical companies themselves, who obviously have an interest in establishing their products. They finance researchers and academics in the field of addiction, supporting them with research grants and consultancy fees. Massive amounts of money have been invested and NRT sales are now about £95 million per year in this country alone, and rising.[1]

Nobody has an equivalent financial interest in the power of the mind. Organisations simply don't exist that could profit in any comparable way by researching and marketing willpower. As a result, the power of the mind tends to get dropped from the picture. This bias permeates many of the professional approaches to most, if not all, addictions. The legacy of the current focus on drug-based therapies is that the development of willpower has been seriously overlooked.

So that we don't ignore the part we play in all of this, a biochemical solution to addiction is a hugely attractive idea and just what many people long for. An easy, guaranteed, magic-bullet cure would surely be a huge success in the modern world. However, just because we want it to happen doesn't mean it will. Just because we would like it to be that way doesn't mean we won't be needing willpower. Not only are pharmaceuticals not the magic answers they might seem to be, the marketing and promotion of them could be creating some additional problems for us.

We expect a 'quick fix' cure

If the way to overcome addiction is through manipulating biochemistry, the responsibility for solving this problem lies with the pharmaceutical companies – and with your doctor. More and more people now expect their doctor, surgery nurse or other health professional to deal with their addiction problem simply by writing out a prescription. Even when a doctor explains that self-control through willpower is what's really needed, many will regard this as a failure of the medical profession. The responsibility is placed on the health-care professional – which means it's not where it belongs, which is with the smoker or with those who are overweight.

This is not just about addiction, of course. Any time we feel below par, a great many of us have come to rely on medication to make us feel better, whether it's over-the-counter painkillers and antacids or something prescribed for more serious symptoms. Pharmaceuticals can save lives, but in general they are used far too much and far too often. All pharmaceuticals have unhealthy side effects. The vast majority do little more than conceal symptoms – quickly and effortlessly – rather than deliver a real cure.

What are the alternatives? Well, there aren't any if what you're after is a quick fix! There's no problem if that really does work for you, but of course it doesn't in most cases in the long term. What works takes more time and effort.

Advice is built around avoidance

As well as NRT, smokers are usually advised to see a counsellor or to join a group for support in stopping smoking – but when they do they are often encouraged to avoid their problem by avoiding circumstances where they might feel tempted, the idea being that if they avoid the circumstances they avoid the temptation.

It's very likely you've come across this kind of advice. If, as a smoker, you smoke while you drink coffee, it's suggested that you drink orange juice instead. Drinking coffee will remind you of smoking and you'll feel tempted. So, you avoid coffee.

This advice is based on the idea that if you avoid temptation for long enough, your body will go through the process of stopping smoking by itself (with or without the aid of NRT). The idea is that your body will cope in much the same way as it might cope with a hangover or a cold. You don't really need to pay much attention to it – except, perhaps, to complain! You take it easy, you take an aspirin and maybe you sleep it off while your body is doing what it needs to do to restore your energy and well-being. You might be advised to drink lots of water, but that, again, is supposed to help the physical process of recovery.

Advice to avoid temptation assumes that your mind doesn't have much of a role to play in the process of breaking free from addiction. The best you can do is to keep your attention on something else if at all possible. Just get your body and brain accustomed to less and less nicotine and allow it to adjust to none at all. And that's it! Except it isn't. In fact, it's doomed to failure – but it's only when you see what a crucial role your mind plays that you can see the value in doing things differently.

Common sense will tell you that avoidance will only work for as long as the situations can be avoided. As soon as you encounter the coffee (or the pub or the phone or whatever) you are faced with the difficulty you've been avoiding. As with any problem in life, it's going to be much better to deal with it.

When you think about it, you are unlikely to be advised to

avoid any other kind of problem that you might have. If you are in debt, for example, a financial adviser is unlikely to tell you to throw away the bills. If you suffer from agoraphobia, you wouldn't be advised to stay at home. You are expected to deal with a difficulty in order to resolve the problem. *Financial problems aren't solved by forgetting about bills, and nobody suggests they are. Nobody overcomes agoraphobia until they begin to face their fears and go outside.*

When it comes to stopping smoking, though, this is often what is recommended, simply because so much of the problem in quitting is regarded as biochemical. This is why smokers aren't usually shown how to think their way through the process of quitting. Some people figure it out for themselves, but many don't.

Those who overeat are often advised along the same lines. If, for example, you eat in front of your TV it's suggested that you get out every evening to avoid temptation. If you eat whenever you feel bored, you keep yourself busy. Unfortunately, when avoidance is your central tool, you set yourself up for failure in the longer term.

Biochemistry rules

Public relations companies work full time to promote pharmaceutical products. They are hired by the pharmaceutical companies and their job is to place articles in the media. These articles often promote the significance of physical addiction, and it seems that every few weeks another gene, hormone or neuro-transmitter has been discovered to play a role, be it in overeating, smoking or any other addiction.

Articles that appear in the press usually follow a format: there's a certain problem for people...this is the science behind it...this is the pharmaceutical that's available now...and this is what they're working on, which will become available in the next few years...and it will work even better...and this is why. As a result, what we hear about in the media most often is the physical, biochemical side of addiction. The public relations companies begin to promote products two or three years before they come on to the market, so there's always the promise of better products in the future. Then, when the new product becomes available, there's already massive interest in it and sales boom.

For example, overweight people find it difficult to stop eating so much. Hunger hormones have been discovered, including one called ghrelin, that tell the brain to stop eating. These hormones create feelings of fullness and satisfaction, and in studies volunteers injected with them eat less food. It is found that obese people have different levels of these hormones from those who are not overweight. They have more of these hunger hormones at the end of a meal, which encourages them to continue eating. Scientists are working on developing a drug that will duplicate these hormones and so eliminate the excess hunger. The bias in this particular media story is something we'll take a look at in our next chapter.

As a result of all this, most people these days have the idea that addiction is caused by biochemistry that's out of control. And when people think about out-of-control biochemistry, it's easy to feel overwhelmed and helpless. The chemical goings-on inside our bodies are completely mysterious to all but a few, but most of us have heard – over and over again – that this is what drives us to smoke or overeat despite our very best intentions.

We are told that we are compelled to pursue our addictions by the actions of chemical messengers in our brains called neurotransmitters. We are encouraged to think in these terms even though most of us don't know what a neurotransmitter is, what it looks like or how to get it to do something really useful like help us to stop smoking or overeating. And so we get stuck in the impossibility of making any real changes on our own. All we can do is wait until the scientists finally get it right and the magic cure arrives.

A Perspective on Pharmaceuticals

Part of the problem with this bias is that some people have become less confident of their own abilities, which undermines self-esteem and, of course, willpower. If a pharmaceutical aid for overcoming addiction doesn't work, many assume they must be hopeless cases. But if pharmaceuticals haven't worked for you in the past, it might be because they aren't as effective as you have been led to believe. Maybe what you need is not another drug – but a greater understanding of how to use your willpower.

No matter what it is you want to use willpower for, if you are already using pharmaceutical support of any kind, or are considering using it in the future, by all means do this. It can help you. But – and this is a very big but – don't expect it to do the work for you. When you come across a pharmaceutical available for your problem, here are some questions to take into consideration.

How effective is it?[2]

It's difficult to evaluate the success rate of NRT that's bought in a pharmacy and used on its own. It's almost impossible to follow people up to see if they actually stopped smoking for even one whole year, which is how success is usually measured. There is some question as to whether NRT works at all in these circumstances. It is thought that perhaps 3 per cent of people benefit, bringing a one-year success rate up from 3 per cent without NRT to 6 per cent with NRT. Many studies, however, have shown that there is more of an improvement in success when smokers use NRT and join a support group as well.

In these studies, groups of smokers trying to quit are divided into two, with half receiving NRT and the other half receiving a placebo. Then, results are compared between them. In the placebo groups, roughly 10 per cent succeed, compared with about 20 per cent of those on NRT. These are the studies where it has been established that NRT is twice as effective as willpower alone.

A great many smokers, however, do not know how to use their willpower. We've already seen in the last chapter that there's a skill to owning choices and we'll cover even more in later chapters about what it takes to use willpower effectively. Volunteers in these trials are not supported in this way. *NRT has never been compared to the effectiveness of showing people how to access their willpower.*

Were the trials really double-blind?[3]

When these studies are conducted, neither the volunteer smokers nor the researchers who interact with them know who is getting the placebo and who is getting the active nicotine in the product being tested. This is called a 'double-blind' trial. The reason for this is because the smokers could be biased if they knew, and if the smokers were biased the trials wouldn't be an objective indication of the biochemical effects of the drug. For the same reason the researchers could give out unconscious messages, perhaps through tone of voice or body language, to suggest to the smokers that the active drug might work better than the placebo. So the researchers aren't told which is which either. People who haven't been involved with the smokers at all gather the data at the end of the trial to evaluate the outcome.

There's a problem, though. For many years researchers have known that a number of people in these trials are aware of whether or not they are getting the active drug. This varies depending on the type of NRT being used. For example, the NRT lozenge delivers nicotine in a way that is more obvious, even though it's far weaker than smoking a cigarette. But whatever type of NRT is being tested, usually far more than the 50 per cent you would expect by chance can say whether or not there is nicotine in the product. In some studies on nicotine patches, 75 per cent could tell.

This awareness influences the success rate. Volunteers, if even slightly aware of the active medication, can become convinced of success and in doing so create success. Even if it makes the crucial difference for only a few, this could account for some of the success – in which case it's the result of an attitude of mind rather than biochemistry. This is important for you to understand if you want to take control of any addictive behaviour. It's important to see what contributes to success: an alteration in biochemistry or a change in attitude.

This glitch in double-blind trials is now being debated by scientists with regard to a great many areas, not just for addictions.[4] Many are now thinking that the placebo effect, which comes from the power of the mind, plays a far more significant role than was previously assumed. This significance is because the placebo effect doesn't apply only to the placebo but to the active pharmaceutical as well. Side effects from the active drug (such as dizziness, dry mouth or insomnia) provide the tip-off, and the stronger the side effects, the more effective the drug seems to be. Much of the effect of any pharmaceutical may be no more than an enhanced placebo response.

Some scientists are beginning to express concern that double-blind, placebo-controlled trials mean that the more toxic a drug is, the more likely it is to 'work'. Which means that more toxic drugs are being released on to the market. Not only are they more toxic – but they only work because we think they will!

Does the success rate include using the pharmaceutical?

In some trials of nicotine gum, 25 per cent of long-term successes were still using it one year later. There's no doubt at all that this is preferable to smoking, as any NRT product is much cleaner and healthier than inhaling smoke. If it's a choice between smoking and NRT, the improved lung function makes NRT an excellent alternative.

However, there are people who get as hooked on NRT as they were on cigarettes and they continue to use it for years – although this is certainly never recommended. Apart from the money it costs, nicotine alone is not good for your health if taken over long periods of time, having been linked to cancer and arterial disease.

A bigger problem is that the pharmaceuticals may only work while they are being taken. This has been a particular problem with Zyban, which can cancel out the desire to smoke. The craving can return when the course of Zyban has been completed, and that's when relapse is most likely. So measuring success while subjects are still taking the medication gives us a distorted picture of success. And one thing to consider is that you could be taking the pharmaceutical for a very long time.

This is especially true for appetite suppressants, as they tend to work only while they are being taken. It's very likely there will be no end to generation after generation of appetite suppressants, all developed to work in different ways on different mechanisms in the body. But it could be that the better they work, the more likely you are to be stuck with them for life.

However, a much bigger problem with appetite suppressants is that the lost weight is more likely to be lean tissue rather than excess storage fat. This is extremely bad news for long-term health and it's also extremely bad news for maintaining the weight loss. The more lean tissue you have, the healthier you are, the younger you stay, and the higher your metabolic rate. Losing lean tissue is the last thing you want to do.

At the very least, find out what kind of weight was lost during the trials. Lean mass loss is mostly due to the fact that a suppressed appetite doesn't necessarily lead to healthy eating. A dinner of one fast-food takeaway instead of three is an improvement in quantity but still doesn't provide the body with the nutrition it needs to maintain its lean mass. Eating in a way that supports your health is a job for willpower, combined with self-esteem. And you'll lose weight too!

Are pharmaceuticals safe?

NRT is possibly the safest pharmaceutical there is. It's been so widely used for such a long time that we would certainly know by now if it ever caused serious problems. There has been some controversy about bupropion (Zyban), although it has now been investigated by the European Medicines Evaluation Agency and given the all-clear. Their conclusion has been that there is no increase in fatalities when taken appropriately. The main problem with Zyban seems to be the fairly unpleasant side effects. In the UK, the Medicines Controls Agency says that of all complaints about medications they have received, one in five has been about side effects from Zyban.

Over the years, one appetite suppressant after another has been pulled off the market, and Reductil is the latest under suspicion. There have been some deaths, it is now thought to raise heart rate and blood pressure, and some consumer groups in the US and Europe have called for it to be banned. Safety problems are difficult to evaluate because the people who are going to be using these medications – smokers and the obese – are not in the best of health to start with. So one side of the argument is that most of the health problems, including deaths, would have happened anyway.

However, just to get some idea of the scale of this problem, it has been estimated that unexpected reactions from medications are the fourth largest cause of death in the United States.[5] This does not include mistakes or overdoses; it is only from taking properly prescribed medications. In an editorial in the *British Medical Journal* recently, doctors were advised to be wary of any newly approved drugs, as an estimated 20 per cent of them are found to have extremely serious side effects which are not picked up until years after they have been put on the market.

Pharmaceuticals can be safe and they can really help. It can be that any health problems from side effects outweigh the risks of continuing to overeat or smoke. The real damage in all of this is that the power of the mind is not only forgotten but consistently invalidated. The myth we live with is that we are all victims of our biochemistry.

Mindpower

I don't think there's any doubt that biochemistry is involved in addictive behaviour. What makes all the difference in how we deal with it is whether or not we acknowledge that our minds, as well as our brains, have power. Consciousness and biochemistry are intimately and powerfully connected – but *our thoughts, feelings and actions are more than simply the automatic expression of one set of chemical processes.*

For example, when a smoker decides to go ahead and do something about stopping smoking, that's a decision they make in their mind, not the result of how much nicotine is in their bloodstream. They decide they've had enough of coughing and feeling exhausted all the time, or they get fed up with all that money they're wasting. They decide they're going to quit and they call their local health centre and sign up for a group. And let's say that when it comes to the first session, they realise it clashes with their favourite TV programme. They need to make a decision about what's important to them and what they will and will not do. It isn't their biochemistry that determines whether they attend the group or stay at home and watch the show, it's their mind. And whether or not they continue to attend that group and stop smoking and whether or not they remain stopped, that also is a series of decisions they make.

When they stop smoking, their biochemistry changes as

nicotine leaves their body. But how difficult it is for them to quit – the anxiety, mood swings and feelings of deprivation they experience – is very much determined by their attitude. As with most things in life, it makes a big difference if they know they have stopped smoking out of their own free will. And later on, perhaps after a few weeks without smoking, what makes the difference between picking up a cigarette and lighting it or not is controlled by a decision made in the mind.

Biochemistry is involved because we only become addicted to things that alter our chemistry in certain crucial ways. It's not a question of whether addiction is a physical *or* a psychological problem. Both are involved. What I plan to show you in the next few chapters is that it's the mind that has the final say. And that's where willpower comes in.

There are some good clues that willpower is the real key to overcoming addiction. One clue is that over the past couple of decades, tens of millions of people have successfully quit smoking. Out of everyone who has ever been a regular smoker, roughly half of them have successfully quit, long term. If nicotine – thought to be the most addictive drug there is – causes loss of self-control, how can this happen? If smokers, once addicted, don't have the choice to quit, how is it that so many are able to do so?

Of these tens of millions of ex-smokers, the overwhelming majority – as many as 85% per cent of them – did it completely on their own. Even those who sought help from hypnotism, acupuncture or NRT may in fact have done it on their own. They used the acupuncture treatment or the course of NRT to get them started, but it's entirely possible that really they used their own willpower to stop. And they used their own will-power to stay stopped in the long term. Using willpower is a completely natural process. Maybe those millions of ex-smok-ers wouldn't be able to explain exactly how – but they had willpower and they used it.

Step by Step

★ **Pay attention to the psychological side of the process** – because this is where the real action lies. Your success depends on how you think. Pharmaceutical support can give you a certain amount of confidence and it can take the edge off some of the discomfort of physical withdrawal, but it doesn't do the job for you. It doesn't give you willpower and it doesn't strengthen your willpower.

★ **Know what it is that's in your way** – If you've found it tough to use willpower effectively, all you need to do is identify what thoughts are blocking you. Change your thinking and you've solved your problem.

★ **Be willing to experience some difficulty in developing willpower** – Magic-cure solutions and the culture that supports them aren't likely to go away, but you can start to give up on the myth of the 'quick fix'. Make using will-power a serious business, make it a priority in your life and something worth spending time on. Put your life at stake (do you think it isn't?) and declare that your life is worth fighting for.

★ **Know that you're worth the time and effort** – because then you can stop waiting for the magic cure and start to take action yourself. It takes real effort to change years of habitual patterns of thinking, and those with lower self-esteem often see it as selfish to put that much attention on themselves. Over the course of a lifetime, those with low self-esteem develop coping strategies to help them feel better about themselves. Often this involves filling their lives up by keeping busy, perhaps in various care-taking roles, so that their attention is continuously on the needs of others. If you recognise yourself in this, and refuse to switch attention to yourself at all, you'll have little opportunity to develop willpower.

★ **If you use pharmaceutical support be especially careful when you finish the course of medication** – as there may well be a higher chance of relapse at this time. This is likely to be because the addictive desire or craving comes back into your mind. It's as if part of the process has been held back, blocked out by the action of the pharmaceutical. This means that the pharmaceutical can give you a helpful start, but it's a big mistake to be completely passive – especially when you stop taking it. That's when you need to do the willpower bit.

★ **Join a support group if you can** – Research shows this improves success rates significantly. Part of the value is in hearing from others in the same boat, knowing you're not alone – and just getting started.

★ **Give your support to a percentage of tax on tobacco to be spent helping smokers quit** – While cigarette prices soar, more and more smokers are among those with lower incomes. If even as little as 2 per cent of tobacco tax was diverted in this way, it would mean more than twice as much help for smokers would become available. Personnel are required, though, not just prescriptions!

★ **Aim to lose fat, not weight** – When someone says they want to lose *weight*, what they really want to do is lose *fat*. The best way to do this is to *increase* lean mass, which is the part of our bodies we are supposed to have. The more lean mass you have, the higher your metabolic rate, the healthier you'll be and the less fat you'll carry. Each pound of muscle burns about thirty-five calories a day, while each pound of fat burns less than two. You increase lean mass by any exercise and by giving your body the nutrition it needs. Lean mass is heavier than fat, so the shift from fat to lean doesn't necessarily show up on the scales. Building lean mass will change the shape of your body, though, as storage fat is lost. Part of the benefit is that you slow down how fast you age. The more lean mass you have, the better.

★ **Educate yourself about nutrition** – I know it's often confusing, but there really are 'good' foods and 'bad' foods. All calories are not equal and it's much too simplistic to think that our bodies work on the basis of calories consumed v. calories used. Nutrient-dense foods are always the better choice, regardless of calorie content. For many people, it can be every bit as much an act of will to eat food that nourishes the body – fruit and vegetables, for example – as to not eat things that are bad for you.

Where There's a Will: Nicky

I had tried to stop smoking many times: through acupuncture, hypnosis and aversion therapy, where they get you to smoke a lot very fast to make you sick of it. I also attended a class in London that was a one-off session, where you throw your cigarettes away and vow never to smoke again. I never used patches or nicotine gum because I knew that, at least for me, the physical withdrawal was virtually nothing.

The hypnosis and acupuncture didn't work for me at all. The aversion therapy was awful; I stopped smoking for a week but substituted alcohol for cigarettes, so it wasn't a good experience. The one-off session I went to was quite good but felt almost like a game, and I think that's why it didn't work. I needed to know if it was a mind trick or not, so I thought I'd test it out and just have one cigarette - and that was it, I was back smoking.

With these therapies, all I could do was trust that they were telling me the truth. It wasn't about me doing it myself. Working this time with Gillian's technique was different; for the first time I felt like I was in the driver's seat. It was more internally driven because I had this idea of having a choice and that it was mine to make. It was a learning process, learning about what I was experiencing. I learned how to make choices by consciously being in the process.

I started smoking when I was 12. I stopped at the age of 37 and had been smoking about 20 a day, although it sometimes varied and I would smoke as much as 30 a day. Now I have not smoked for about six months and feel very much in control. I really like being free from smoking and it's very straightforward for me not to smoke.

Notes

1. Many multinational companies have larger (and therefore more powerful) economies than some of the countries they do business in. Pharmaceutical giant GlaxoSmithKline, for example, has an economy equal in size to Syria. Reported in the *Financial Times*, 13 August 2002.

2. The antidepressant bupropion (Zyban) seems to be more effective than NRT, with the average over all trials conducted so far showing a 10 per cent improvement over a placebo, according to the National Institute for Clinical Excellence, (*Guidance on the use of nicotine replacement therapy and bupropion for smoking cessation*, March 2002.) However, this could at least partly be the result of an enhanced placebo effect created by very noticeable side effects (see the next section on the double-blinding of trials). A major review from California, published in the *Journal of the American Medical Association* (288; 1260-1264, 2002) concluded that NRT products 'were not associated with a clinically meaningful long-term improvement in successful cessation, and no benefit was observed for light (15 a day or less) smokers.'

3. In studies of antidepressants, as many as 80 per cent of volunteers knew whether they were taking the active drug or a placebo. On average, between 70 and 80 per cent of subjects in any kind of trial correctly guessed which they were taking. A paper published in the *Journal of Nervous and Mental Diseases* (181;345–350, 1993) concludes: 'The available data suggest that one has good reason to entertain serious doubts about the integrity of the double-blind trial in any study unless it specifically provides reassuring information that the participants were not able to penetrate the design.'

4. 'The placebo effect exploits the fact that our bodies are dynamic systems that are sensitive to our thoughts and state of consciousness... The worse the side effects, the more likely you are to believe you are getting the drug. This could trigger a placebo response, artificially boosting the drug's performance. In effect, a drug that is boosted by a placebo response is being compared with a "placebo" with less placebo effect.' (*Medicine Today*, July 2001.)

5. 'The incidence of serious and fatal adverse drug reactions in US hospitals was found to be extremely high.' Published in the *Journal of the American Medical Association* (279, April 1998). Editorial in the *British Medical Journal* (324, May 2002): 'Doctors warned to be wary of new drugs.'

CHAPTER FIVE

Mind Yourself

The chemistry of addiction and the impact of your mind

Here, as clearly and briefly as possible, is some of the current thinking on the biochemistry of addiction. This is about how addiction is explained in terms of the physical effects of drugs. This is not about the ill health caused by an addiction, such as damage to the lungs and heart from smoking or problems with insulin metabolism from addictive overeating. This is about the chemistry that turns a mere habit into an addiction.

The things we become addicted to – including sugar, caffeine and nicotine, as well as illegal drugs such as cocaine and heroin – all have the potential to become addictions because of the effect they have on our biochemistry, especially of our brains. Obviously, there are major differences in these effects. Smoking a cigarette is not the same as smoking crack cocaine. Eating sweets is not the same as taking amphetamines. But it is thought that all of these can become addictive largely because of their various effects on neurotransmitters, which are the chemical signals between the neurons (cells) in our brains. They dramatically increase the levels of the neurotransmitters or in some cases they mimic them by duplicating their effects.

People don't usually become addicted to smoking herbal cigarettes, drinking water or eating celery, the reason being that these things don't have this effect on our brain chemistry. You've no doubt heard the names of some of these neurotransmitters: dopamine, serotonin and beta-endorphin. Often referred to as 'reward chemicals' or 'feel-good chemicals', they produce positive feelings of relaxation, confidence, energy and even euphoria. They make us feel cosy, happy and alert. These feelings of satisfaction and security are what we all yearn for, so it's no wonder we repeat them. And repeat. And repeat. And repeat.

For exactly the same reasons, some people can become hooked on activities such as gambling, shopping and exercise. Neurotransmitters are generated by our own bodies, and for some people the anticipation and excitement of these activities creates a rush or 'hit' of these chemicals, rather than a steady dose at a steady pace. The experience of sexual orgasm is created by a sudden rush of dopamine, so it's easy to see why we get so interested in seeking out ways to simulate this excitement.

The role of these chemicals is to reinforce natural, life-enhancing behaviours, so that activities such as having sex and eating food are rewarding for us. These chemicals encourage us to support our lives and the life of our species. An addiction is like a parasite that exploits this natural and beneficial reward system. It does this by rewarding us for behaviours such as smoking and overeating (especially sugar and processed wheat) that are actually bad for us.

There are some important details which will help us in our use of willpower:

★ The addicting drugs create their effects when they move from the bloodstream into the neurons in the brain. The neurons get too much of these chemicals all at once, so they adapt to the excess by increasing their number and, at the same time, by becoming less sensitive.

★ When the chemical reaction has become desensitised, you are left seeking the initial or occasional high or buzz, which tends to fade with more use.

★ These changes in the brain persist; some of them are permanent and best thought of as a scar. The brain and the way it works have been physically altered by the addicting drugs. This is what is meant when a smoker is said to be 'physically dependent' and that addiction is a 'chronic disease'.

The popular view of addiction is that when someone tries to quit, their brain needs the fix of chemicals it has become accustomed to. Your brain has had its regular dose of some version of the chemistry described above, possibly for many years. When you use willpower and take control of the addiction, that chemistry stops happening. The brain chemistry gets very upset and unbalanced, and you experience the misery, the agony and the general mayhem of physical withdrawal as a direct result. You crave, you rage, you grieve and your life falls apart.

There's a problem with this, though, and the problem is that it doesn't take into account the impact of the way we think, the attitudes and beliefs we hold in our mind. This impact is huge, and to get some idea of how huge it is, let's take a look at some interesting research.

Two-Way Communication

A group of smokers who had volunteered to take part in a study were asked not to smoke for twelve hours before coming into the research centre where this study was being conducted.[1] Each one was interviewed and asked many questions about how they were feeling and how much they wanted to smoke a cigarette. They had already been identified as being 'highly dependent' smokers so, as you can imagine, there was no doubt they really did want to smoke. After twelve hours of not smoking at all, they were beginning to experience symptoms of withdrawal such as irritability, restlessness, anxiety and strong cravings. After the interview, they smoked a cigarette

and then described how much better they felt, and how satisfying that cigarette was for them. So at the end of all this, there
was a great deal written down about the thoughts and feelings
of the smokers before and after smoking a cigarette.

You might at this point be wondering about how some
people make a living, but there is a point to all this! A week
later, the procedure was repeated with the same group of
smokers. They were asked not to smoke for twelve hours and
when they arrived they were given the same questionnaire.
Then they were given a cigarette to smoke before doing the
next questionnaire, so that there was a record of how their
withdrawal symptoms went away, how good they felt after
smoking, how great that cigarette was and how much it satisfied their craving. Except that the second time, the cigarette
didn't have any nicotine in it. It was made of tobacco and it felt
and tasted and smelled just like a real cigarette, but the nicotine – which we all know is the addicting drug in cigarettes –
had been chemically removed.

The punch line is that the responses to the questionnaires
were virtually identical. The normal cigarettes with nicotine
and cigarettes with no nicotine were almost as good as each
other in reducing the withdrawal symptoms. Just to make sure,
a blood sample was taken and it confirmed that when the nicotine-free cigarettes had been smoked, no nicotine had entered
the bloodstream. Even though these smokers had received no

nicotine at all in their blood and in their brain, their craving was satisfied and physical feelings of withdrawal subsided.

The researchers behind this study point out that this effect is 'subject to rapid extinction', which is their way of saying that you can't keep it going for very long. Fairly soon the smokers would realise there was something wrong with the cigarettes and the effect would disappear. But the fact that it happens at all, even for a brief period of time, gives us a very clear indication of what the mind can do. We can begin to see the difference made by attitude in the process of addiction. The smokers expected to feel better after they smoked the cigarette, and so they did!

Another study points us in the same direction using very different methods.[2] In this study, a group of twenty-a-day smokers were asked to smoke cigarettes after having rinsed their mouths and gargled with an anaesthetic. This meant they couldn't feel any of the sensations of smoking in their mouths and throats. A control group of smokers gargled with something that didn't have any anaesthetic effect, so that results could be compared. The point is that if smoking is all about getting nicotine into the system and getting those neurotransmitters going, it shouldn't matter too much whether or not the smoker is aware of the feeling of smoke going down their throat. As long as nicotine is delivered to those brain cells, that should be enough. But it isn't. The smokers with anaesthetised throats didn't even want to finish their cigarettes and didn't particularly want another when it was offered, in sharp contrast to the control group. The reduction in craving is described in this study as dramatic.

These effects are not confined to smokers.[3]

★ One researcher took the active ingredients – the 'drugs' – from chocolate and fed them to chocoholic volunteers in the form of a pill. They weren't in the least bit interested in the pill and it did nothing to satisfy their craving for the real thing.

★ In one study, alcoholics were given heavily disguised cocktails containing one ounce of 100 per cent proof vodka. Half of the group were told that there was alcohol in their drinks and the other half were told that there wasn't. Only those who knew they had consumed alcohol wanted to drink more. Those who had been told their drinks were alcohol-free were not at all interested in a second round.

★ In a study of overeaters, fifty people with 'binge eating disorder' were recruited for a trial and given a placebo for four weeks before they started the active medication that was being evaluated. Binge eating fell by an average of 72 per cent – from six to fewer than two episodes a week – during the placebo period. Twenty-two of the group became ineligible for the trial because they were no longer experiencing the required disorder.

There is really only one way to make sense of research like this, and that is to acknowledge that while the chemistry of our bodies has an effect on the mind, our thoughts and beliefs also have an effect on our bodies. A few years ago I came across an excellent way to understand this when I went to a lecture given by Dr Herbert Benson, one of the world's leading experts on mind–body medicine. Dr Benson is one of those all-too-rare individuals who have immersed themselves in the fields of both modern, physical medicine and the significance of mind and spirit. An Associate Professor of Medicine at Harvard Medical School, he is the Founder and President of their Mind–Body Medical Institute.

What I found so helpful to apply to our understanding of addiction is his use of the terms 'bottom-up' and 'top-down' to describe the relationship between body and mind:

★ **Bottom-up** – refers to physical events taking place in the body which you then become aware of in your mind. Burning your finger is an example of a bottom-up experience.

★ **Top-down** – refers to thoughts – either memories or new thoughts – that create a response in the body and the brain. If, when you remembered burning your finger, you felt a bit of the pain again, that's an example of a top-down experience.

Dr Benson is especially well known for research into meditation, which provides us with another good example. Meditation produces physical changes, and this has been very well established in studies as it can be very easily measured. When a person meditates, their body consumes less oxygen, their metabolic rate slows down, their heart rate slows, blood pressure lowers and the sympathetic nervous system is inhibited. Meditation also creates more alpha waves in the brain, which are the slower brain waves. This is why meditation has such a positive effect on levels of stress. The effects are similar to sleep but different in many crucial details. Meditators do not simply snooze; there is a unique quality to meditation which cannot be achieved by other means. It's just one example of the effect the mind has on the body.

Choosing to meditate is a decision made in the mind. It is an act of will – and the effects show up in the body. This is what Dr Benson calls a top-down event. It doesn't end there, though, because the physical effects from meditating then show up in the mind. Having practised meditation, you become aware in your mind that your thinking is more clear, and you feel more relaxed and refreshed.

No matter how you lower your level of stress – by meditating, doing yoga, taking a long walk or going on a good holiday – you have probably experienced how much better you feel as a result, and how you are able to think more clearly and calmly. This is the bottom-up side of it. The mind has an effect on the body. And the body has an effect on the mind.

Seeing how this works with meditation is helpful, but don't get the idea that this is only relevant in certain specialised activities and only in terms of relaxation. Mind and body are in continuous, two-way communication. They are inseparable. Their communication continues all the time – whether we are aware of it or not – twenty-four hours a day, seven days a week, throughout our entire lives.

Automatic or Deliberate

The influence of the mind on the body happens in many different ways. Top-down events can be deliberately chosen, as in meditation, or they can be quite unconscious and automatic. They can be passing effects, gone in seconds, or they can last much longer.

For example, I can deliberately create a brief top-down experience in the comfort of my own living room! I love to ride roller-coasters, and I can close my eyes and imagine myself at the top of that first, highest peak on my favourite ride. As I begin my imaginary descent, my stomach lurches just as it would do if I was really there, hurtling downwards. The feeling is not as strong as the real thing but it's certainly very similar. This is because my brain is working in a similar way as it would if I was there. If there were scientists there in my living room they would be able to measure the effect my mind was having on my body.

More often, though, top-down events are so familiar they become automatic and not at all deliberately chosen. There are a massive number of examples in our lives. One you may know about is that when a doctor takes a patient's blood pressure, the patient's way of thinking actually sends the blood pressure up.[4] This way of thinking, which probably includes some fearful and anxious thoughts, produces a stronger reaction when a doctor takes the blood pressure than when a nurse does it! Many patients, it seems, have particular beliefs about doctors, and these thoughts have top-down, physical effects.

The placebo effect is another example, as it relies on the confidence that's assumed in the power of a pill. People don't consciously choose to recover with a placebo; in fact, the effect happens when they don't even know they're taking one. Phobias and anxiety disorders are largely automatic; agoraphobics don't deliberately feel terrified when they open their front doors.

How do we know, then, that there is a top-down influence on these experiences at all? We know because phobias and anxiety disorders respond extremely well to cognitive therapy, which is a form of counselling that enables people to re-evaluate the thinking behind their fears. Cognitive therapy helps people to let go of fearful thoughts, and as a result, the physical feelings of anxiety and fear begin to fade. Pharmaceuticals such as anti-depressants can help, but cognitive therapy is now seen to be crucial and highly effective. Since mind and body communicate continuously – thoughts affect the body, body chemistry affects thoughts – top-down and bottom-up solutions are sometimes used together.

In the example of depression, a pessimistic state of mind has an influence on biochemistry, which in turn influences the negative state of mind. The Prozac style of anti-depressants work by getting more serotonin to stay in these neurons, but cognitive therapy – a change of attitude – is not only essential but has proved to be more effective than pharmaceuticals. Depression doesn't develop *purely* as a result of low levels of the reward chemicals in the brain. One theory about this is that anti-depressants work temporarily, but if the top-down attitude isn't changed, the brain compensates for the medication so that it stops working after a while. Another theory is that anti-depressants work very largely through a placebo effect. In other words, it's the top-down state of mind, the belief that this medication will improve things, that makes much of the difference.[5]

The effect of mind on body can last a lifetime.[6] There's strong evidence that those who keep their minds active are less likely to suffer from the brain diseases associated with ageing. There's the evidence from a number of studies that optimists live longer and healthier lives than those who tend to be pessimistic. There's an enormous amount of evidence for the ways in which our mind alters our biochemistry. This is especially interesting for us in looking at willpower and addiction.

Mind Over Matter – *and* Matter Over Mind

First of all, let's take a look at hunger, which is often assumed to be a purely bottom-up experience. We think of hunger as bottom-up because we think it's the way our body tells us we need to eat something. This is very important to understand, because those who are overweight eat too much food mostly because they get hungry much too often. Get rid of the excess hunger and you get rid of the overeating – which, in turn, gets rid of the excess weight.

There is such a thing as genuine, natural hunger but it is rarely, if ever, experienced by overeaters, simply because they don't wait long enough for it to appear. Instead, they feed a top-down hunger, one in which *the mind creates chemistry that's virtually identical to the real thing.*[7]

We know this through studies of people and animals where we can see that hunger can be easily attached to cues. There are many examples. Rats hear a bell ring whenever they eat, which trains them to associate that particular sound with food. Then, *even when they are full,* they eat more food whenever they hear the bell. The famous experiments by the scientist Ivan Pavlov demonstrated that dogs salivated on cue once they had learned to associate food with a bell or a flashing light.

One unusual experiment with human subjects was carried out not with overeaters, but with two men with severe short-term memory loss.[8] These men were invited into the research centre on the pretext of conducting some studies on memory. They did some routine experiments and halfway through the day someone from the team brought them a delicious three-course lunch, which the men ate. Thirty minutes later, with all evidence of the lunch removed, the team brought in an identical meal and the men, having forgotten they had already had lunch, ate all of it again. The process was repeated a third time and it was only on the fourth occasion, when the men had eaten three full lunches, that they refused the food, explaining that they felt a little bit full. This entire procedure was repeated on three consecutive days.

Their appetite was stimulated simply because they believed it was time for lunch. They had no memory of having just eaten – *and their bodies weren't giving them very good clues.*

Along with extra salivation, the cue to eat triggers production of insulin in the bloodstream, digestive acids in the stomach and a corresponding fall in blood sugar levels. The cue is your anticipation of food, the thought that you are about to eat something tasty, and it also triggers the release of dopamine in the brain. This happens *before* you eat *anything*.[9]

All of this biochemistry then creates a bottom-up event where your body tells your mind you're hungry. If you usually respond to this by eating, you reinforce the cue one more time. Then, the next time you encounter that cue you feel addictive hunger or craving again. And on and on it goes. Remember, your mind has an effect on your body and your body has an effect on your mind – and this communication never stops, not for a second.

The cues that start this cycle off can be absolutely anything – including the time of day, particular places (such as your car or living room sofa) and emotional states (such as anger or boredom). All that's needed is for you to have created an asso-ciation between food and the cue by eating in that circum-stance in the past – especially if you repeated it a few times. It also applies to the 'hunger' that's experienced at the end of a meal. If it is usually fed, it too becomes reinforced.

Now we can see the bias in those media stories on pharma-ceutical interventions, such as the ones about the hunger hormones mentioned in our last chapter. What they fail to mention is the top-down effect of mind on body chemistry. They don't tell you that the body chemistry responds to the expectation of more food simply because it has been trained to – and that you can train it in new ways. How you make the changes by using your mind instead is all about the correct use of willpower, which we'll get to in our next chapter.

For the same reasons, smokers feel their desire to smoke on cue. That desire is felt as a physical sensation; heart rate increases slightly and some smokers even produce extra salivation when they want to smoke. Let's say a teenager has his first few cigarettes at a friend's house. So, when he goes back to visit his friend, the surroundings are his cue to smoke and he feels like smoking a cigarette again. His mind affects his body as he feels his craving for another 'hit' of nicotine. He satisfies the craving by smoking another cigarette, which reinforces the cue one more time.

The mind has an effect on the body – but the body also has an effect on the mind. Smoking a cigarette is a bottom-up event. Smoke enters the body and nicotine enters the bloodstream, causing a multitude of chemical reactions, including the release of insulin and adrenaline, causing an increase in heart rate, and the mimicking of dopamine in the brain, which creates a sense of pleasure. For a brief moment (about one second!) the smoker's *mind* is satisfied, energised and happy.

Most people can easily see that their addictive desire is connected to cues, but also that it's more than an ordinary memory. You don't simply recall that you smoked a cigarette when you were there before, in the same way that you might remember what you were wearing that day or that it was raining at the time. Remember that scar in the brain? That's what turns simply remembering the cigarette into an addictive desire.

Addictive desire is a product of this interaction between body and mind.[10] Both play crucial roles, so any focus on the biochemistry of addiction is limited to only one part of the whole picture. Taking control of addiction is not simply a matter of allowing the body and brain to adjust and recover. And it's not just a matter of adding or subtracting hormones and neurotransmitters to get the right balance of biochemicals.

If you ignore the influence of your mind in this process, you not only miss out on your most powerful resource but you are simply not going to be able to take control of that aspect. No matter what is going on with your body chemistry, you make things much more difficult than they need to be if you don't learn how to use willpower.

Stupid Machines

There will always be limitations to a purely biochemical solution to addiction because it's based on a relatively simplistic, mechanical description of the body. Thinking of our bodies as machines has been the main focus of medicine for hundreds of years – and it has brought us a very long way. It's true there are a great many ways in which we seem mechanical, with particular causes creating particular, predictable effects. Our hearts seem to work like pumps, our muscles appear to be systems of pulleys and our brains are often compared to computers. All of the successful conventional medicine we see around us today is based on this mechanical view. This is how most of us think about medicine and this is how our health professionals have been trained to think.

Antibiotics and vaccines work along these lines. The control of diabetes through insulin injections is a mechanical process. A chemical is missing, so we replace it. Surgery is a mechanical concept. We can easily see the comparison between an organ transplant and the work a mechanic would perform on our car. Each area of our body is seen as separate, which is why separate specialities have developed in modern medicine.

However, there are many health problems which have not responded so well to mechanical cures. Addiction would be top of a list that would also include heart disease, diabetes and all the stress-related problems such as chronic fatigue, irritable bowel syndrome and insomnia. Sometimes symptoms can be controlled through conventional medications, but cures appear to be far more complicated and out of reach of the mechanical models. For a long time we were sold on the idea of dealing with the difficulties of the menopause in an entirely mechanistic way. Women lose oestrogen at this time in their lives, creating symptoms such as hot flushes. So, you replace the oestrogen and you've solved the problem. Except that we now know it's not that simple.[11]

There are aspects of our bodies that seem mechanical but there are also major differences. For one thing, machines don't grow from eggs to adult-sized versions. When they get broken, they don't repair themselves. And they don't have feelings, opinions, attitudes and expectations.

What is now beginning to emerge is the image not of a mindless machine, but of an intricate network. This image is of an extraordinarily complex communications system, one which operates on many different levels at once, and all of them interconnected and in communication. The whole system is far greater than any of the parts – and the mind has an influence on it all.

Thinking of the body and the brain as simplistic machines is outdated – *and yet it's important to realise that most of us still do this*. It's our legacy from the past, from medicine and science over the past few generations. Hundreds of years ago mind and spirit were regarded as central to health and illness. Then, when mechanical medicine began to work so well, the baby got thrown out with the bath-water. We discovered what to do about the mechanical actions of germs and viruses, and the role of the mind began to be regarded as nothing more than superstition. Body and mind were separated, and the mind has been more and more disregarded in favour of our modern machines.

If our machine-body doesn't think, then the medications that cure it can be mindless as well. The role of our beliefs, of the way we think and feel, is ignored. We've all learned to think this way but it's got us all into a big muddle – especially in the treatment of addiction.

Top-Down Addiction

I once saw a brilliant BBC TV show which demonstrated very powerfully the extraordinary impact of mind over body. It was called *Trust Me, I'm a Doctor* and it was good to see it on TV because you could actually watch it all happening in front of your eyes. I hope I can describe it well enough to you in words.

A group of twenty-somethings were taken to a pub, having been invited to take part in a demonstration of the effects of alcohol. They were asked to drink glasses of vodka and orange juice, all at the same time and at the same rate. As the evening wore on, they took a number of different tests which had been set up in the pub to measure the effects on coordination and reaction time. As you would expect, their performance got steadily worse and worse over the evening as more and more drinks were consumed. And as you would expect, the conversations in the group got more and more animated and flirtatious. Their faces became flushed and they wobbled a lot more when asked to balance on one leg. A computer game showed that their reaction times had slowed down by a third.

Then, the real point of the exercise was revealed: no alcohol had been served at all. They got drunk simply because they *believed* they were getting drunk. Maybe you think you would have known that there was no alcohol in the drink, and I'm sure at some point somebody would have twigged. This sort of thing needs to be very convincingly set up, and even then the illusion is not likely to last long. As with those smokers and their nicotine-free cigarettes, removing alcohol from our drinks isn't going to work in the longer term. What's interesting about it, though, is that this happens at all, even for an hour or two.

Whenever I think of this extraordinary illustration of what the mind can do, I always think about withdrawal symptoms, especially when people stop smoking. There's no doubt a chemical basis for these symptoms – but the mind takes them and exaggerates them beyond all recognition. It could be that smokers crave, get angry, hungry and depressed when they quit at least partly because they expect to. Then, what would have been fairly mild and very temporary changes in biochemistry become a dramatic, continuing drama.

In this experiment and those about the smokers I mentioned at the beginning of this chapter, people have been tricked into believing something. This shows us how the way you are thinking influences how you feel and act. But willpower is yours when you start to change your attitude deliberately. This is not trickery. It's clear, honest thinking – and knowing which attitudes to question and revise.

Addiction is not, as many people suggest, 'all in the mind'. Addiction means your brain has had an experience of a particular drug. It bears the scar, so the memory of addiction persists in the form of addictive desire. That's the bad news. The good news is that you can choose your response to that memory. You can either take the attitude that you're hopelessly, chemically dependent and controlled by your chemistry, or the attitude that this is why you need to put some power behind your will. The really good news happens when you choose this second option, because the power behind your will has a direct effect on healing the addiction. This is what we'll look at next.

Step by Step

★ **Get the best equipment for the job** – When it comes to using willpower, your equipment is your body. The better you look after it, the better it will perform for you, so pay attention to the quality and quantity of your sleep, water, food, exercise and stress. Higher levels of antioxidants and water, for example, create better brain function, which becomes more noticeable as you get older. This is about creating higher levels of physical energy and mental clarity, which will support you in doing what you are setting out to accomplish. It even makes a difference to what you might want to tackle in the first place, as someone in poor health may be less likely to want to set bigger challenges for themselves. Even moderate improvements in levels of health, vitality and energy can make a contribution to your use of willpower.

★ **Notice 'top-down' events** – such as addictive hunger and addictive desire to smoke. You will no doubt feel them in your body, but you can see they start out as thoughts because they are triggered by familiar cues.

★ **Notice what physical symptoms you get when you use willpower** – and remember that just because you feel things physically doesn't mean they have entirely physical causes. An increase in irritability or depression is mostly created by the mind. This is not a deliberate act. People don't consciously choose to get angry or depressed, but an attitude that denies free choice will blow things out of proportion. As this is created by attitude, it can only be reversed by a revised attitude – see Chapter Three on how.

★ **Notice your expectations** – because it's very possible they will come true. What is it that you expect to happen when you use willpower to take control? Some people believe they always overeat whenever they quit smoking. This belief could create the extra hunger they feel. Some people 'know' they get depressed whenever they cut back on their addictive overeating. And so they do. What are you likely to create?

★ **Deliberately develop a more positive state of mind** – If anti-depressants work mostly through the unconscious placebo effect, it follows that you could simply will yourself to become more optimistic. Perhaps, at least to some extent, happiness is a choice, and like any other choice, the more we repeat it the more natural it seems and the easier it is to choose. Do you tend to see your glass as half-empty or half-full? It's your choice! I'm not suggesting that you put on a 'happy face' when inside your heart is breaking. I do suspect, though, that for a great many people much can be gained by choosing to appreciate what they already have and who they already are.

★ **Start to question any labels you give yourself** – that you tend to assume are part of who you are. For example, you may think of yourself as being someone who is hungry all the time, of being a chocoholic or a born smoker. It could be that these things aren't as cast in stone as you think. It could be that your conviction in them reinforces them, when a change in attitude would make a big difference. If you want to make a change, start out by simply refusing to describe yourself this way, either to yourself or to others.

★ **Use reason, logic and knowledge** – to decide what to eat, when to eat and when to stop. Your body signals for hunger and fullness are unreliable, easily misinterpreted and often over-ridden by habitual cues from the past. Also, it makes no sense to rely on natural instincts when we don't treat our bodies in the ways they were designed for, in terms of both the exercise we take and the kind of food we eat. In addition, stress will eliminate sensations of natural hunger because the 'fight or flight' response diverts blood away from the stomach and slows down the digestive process. You can end up undereating if you wait for natural hunger to appear. You can end up overeating if you confuse addictive hunger with the real thing.

Where There's a Will: Andrew

Whenever anybody says they have a physical addiction to cigarettes, I think, yes, but I suspect that their mind needs it a lot more than their body does. In my own experience of stopping smoking, the physical side of it, the twitchiness of wanting to keep on picking up cigarettes, only lasted a couple of days. It was intense and sometimes it would come back when there was a reminder, when I would see someone smoking or when I picked up the phone at work. The physical anxiety became a lot less very quickly. It was dealing with my mind that was harder, particularly the idea of 'Go on just have one, it will just be one and I won't have any more.' But I knew from experience, because I had tried many times before, that it wouldn't be just one.

I stopped smoking after reading *How to Stop Smoking and Stay Stopped for Good* and that was about five years ago. Smoking is very self-destructive, and you know it's a self-destructive thing you are doing, so you're kidding yourself about it and that's not a nice place to be. You know you are playing Russian roulette with your life. These days I still appreciate the cash I save and the freedom from the addiction.

My wife and I had two nights in Barcelona recently, leaving the kids behind with their grandparents. It was a very unusual situation for us. We were put up in a five-star hotel and given loads of fantastic food and wine. Staying up late at night was just like the partying lifestyle of my youth, and it brought back some feelings of desire for cigarettes. I really wanted to smoke! I kept thinking to myself, 'Go on have one, it's been so long now it will be fine.' I think that because I had the practice, the willpower bit was more instinctive. I had those thoughts but I have become very used to not smoking in response to them. It's like that is what is embedded in my thinking now, and so 'Go on and have one' is a thought I have sometimes but it simply doesn't convince me any more.

Notes

1. 'The regular and de-nic cigarettes were equivalent in reducing acute withdrawal symptoms.' Published in *Pharmacology, Biochemistry and Behavior* (50;91–96, 1995), 'Smoking without nicotine delivery decreases withdrawal in 12-hour abstinent smokers.'

2. Published in *Addictive Behaviours* (9;211–215, 1984), 'Subjective response to cigarette smoking following airway anesthetization.'

3. Dr Paul Rozin conducted this chocolate study and concluded that 'people like chocolate because it tastes good'. The study with alcoholics was reported in *Appetite* (1990; 15, 231–246) and concluded: 'This demonstration as well as others indicates that craving depends as much upon one's cognitions as on one's physiological or pharmacological experiences.' The study of binge eaters was published in the *International Journal of Obesity* (20, 1–6, 1996).

4. A Southampton University study of 200 patients found that the 'white-coat effect' triggers falsely high readings of blood pressure for thousands of patients. Reported in the *British Medical Journal*, August 2002.

5. 'In many randomized controlled trials the response associated with placebo is similar to that associated with an established antidepressant.' *Journal of the American Medical Association* (April 2002, 287;14), 'Placebo response in studies of major depression.'

A study at the Royal Free and University College Medical School in London compared patients receiving counselling with those on anti-depressants, and concluded that patients got better faster with counselling and that it was more cost-effective (*Medicine Today*, January 2001).

6. One study published in the *Mayo Clinic Proceedings* (77(8);748–753, 2002) concluded that a pessimistic style was significantly associated with poorer physical and mental functioning thirty years later. A Yale University team followed 660 people over twenty-three years and concluded that 'The effect of more positive self-perceptions of aging on survival is greater than the physiological measures of low systolic blood pressure and cholesterol...positive self-perceptions can prolong life expectancy' (*Journal of the American Psychological Association*, July 2002).

7. Some of this information is taken from a paper published in *Addictive Behaviors* (15;387–393, 1990) by Jane Wardle at the Institute of Psychiatry, University of London.

8. This experiment was conducted by Professor Paul Rozin at the University of Pennsylvania, and reported in *The New Yorker*, July 2001.

9. 'The increase in dopamine is small but measurable.' (Synapse 44;175–180, 2002), 'Dopamine (causes) the cue to increase the motivational state of "wanting" the reward...'

10. For example, studies have established that asking smokers to hold a lit cigarette generates a far stronger urge to smoke compared to when the cigarette is unlit. Three such studies are referred to in a research report in *Addiction* (96;1419–1432, 2001).

11. Simplistic mechanism has led us astray with regard to osteoporosis, as it has now been suggested that supplementing with calcium might actually *speed up* the thinning of bones. There is so much more to take into consideration, including the acid/alkaline balance of our bodies, and the balance of other minerals such as phosphorus, zinc, magnesium and copper. The phosphorus content in fizzy drinks, for example, leads to a five times higher risk of bone fractures in teenage girls (*Medicine Today*, August 2000 and October 2002).

CHAPTER SIX

The Best
Way Out

Using willpower to retrain your brain

When you experience addictive desire you are facing everything that's difficult about using willpower. Addictive desire is any sense of attraction for your addictive behaviour, any urge you feel, ranging all the way from fleeting whim to intense craving and addictive hunger. Addictive desire can seem as trivial as a hiccup or it can be a deep longing and constant obsession.

No matter what form it takes, whenever you experience your addictive desire, you can satisfy it or you can use willpower to take control of your actions. This chapter is all about the second option.

Addictive craving can feel overwhelming, and is what makes addiction so tough to control. However, addiction can be controlled, and the key is to understand the top-down aspect of craving, the part that's created by the mind and can be changed by the mind. This is the key, because when you change the way you think, you not only make things easier for yourself, you vastly increase your chances of long-term success.

Friend or Foe?

When trying to use willpower for self-control, most people think their addictive desire is the enemy. Here you are wanting to change your ways, quit smoking, go on a diet, or whatever. Then along comes a feeling of addictive desire, and suddenly you find yourself in a conflict. You want to indulge – but at the same time you've been wanting to control this urge. Conflict is not a happy place to be, so the addictive desire is seen as a major problem. You fear that it has power over you to make you do things you'll regret. If only it would go away, you'd be able to succeed in your good intentions.

A great many professionals in the field of addiction support this view, and most addiction counsellors would agree that it's best to eliminate addictive desire if at all possible. The general view is that addictive desire *causes* the addictive behaviour, so if you eliminate the desire you eliminate the behaviour. So, most of the advice you hear is built around this aim of getting rid of it.

We have already looked at some of the common avoidance strategies, in Chapter Four. You'll often be told to block out thoughts of your drug of addiction, to keep yourself busy and concentrate on something else. Take a bath, phone a friend, read a book, go for a run – do anything but let yourself feel your addictive desire. Even the common advice to wait it out still regards the desire as a problem. If it can't be avoided, the best you can do is to think of it as a pain to be tolerated. And for exactly the same reasons, pharmaceuticals are effective for addictions to the extent that they take away the addictive desire, craving or hunger.

Counselling for addictive overeating is usually based on this premise. Those people who lack control over food are often encouraged to delve into the emotions and issues that are assumed to drive their overeating. The theory is that once these emotions are owned and the issues resolved, the addictive hunger evaporates. The assumption is, again, that addictive desire should be eliminated.

Most people think of addictive desire as the enemy, but this is the attitude to turn on its head. When you do, everything changes.

Top-Down Healing

First of all, let's remember how addictive desire was created in the first place. As we saw in the last chapter, addictive desire is developed over time by reinforcing the associations between your addiction and particular cues. Whenever a cue reminds you of your past addictive behaviour, this memory is your addictive desire. Whenever you satisfied your desire, you rein-forced it, which strengthened the connection with that cue once again. So, for example, if you smoke cigarettes in your coffee break, you'll want to smoke when you take the break.

The interesting part is how you go about changing things. When you encounter those cues and you don't satisfy the addic-tive desire, the association fades and so the addictive desire fades, rapidly becoming far more manageable. So when you first stop smoking, you drink a cup of coffee and expect to feel your desire to smoke. You then allow yourself to feel that desire.

This is where the real breakthrough happens, when you start to face addictive desire and see it as the way you make change possible. It isn't just your attitude that changes – *this physically changes your brain as well.*

This process is fairly well understood, although, for reasons we'll look at in a moment, it has yet to gain popularity with those who treat addictions of various kinds. The development of relatively new brain-scanning technology has made it possi-ble for us to see that whenever an area of the brain is used repeatedly, it becomes physically larger, stronger and more active. And when an area is not used, it weakens. One of the best-known examples of this top-down effect on the brain is that of London taxi drivers, whose brain scans showed a larger-than-average area associated with memories of how to get to places.[1] London taxi drivers need to remember the vast maze of routes they cover, and this daily mental activity actually makes that part of their brain grow larger.

Of course the details are complicated, but all that you and I need to understand is fairly simple and straightforward.[2] Our ways of thinking are created when groups of cells in our brains (neurons) team up and work together at the same time. The way these cells work is to send electrical signals (via neurotransmitters) from one to another, over tens of thousands of cells. When these signals have been repeated a few times the cells involved link up and establish a particular pattern of connections between them. Then the signals are more likely to follow that pattern in future and the end result is that something has been remembered. We have made a connection – quite literally – in our brains. And the more that particular connection is used, the stronger it gets.

Remember, though, that when it comes to the memory of something that's addictive, this pattern has not only been reinforced through repetition but also through the influence of the addicting drugs on the neurotransmitters. A reward is involved, so our brain thinks our survival is at stake. So the memory is more strongly bonded, which means we have a stronger, more persistent memory and an experience of addictive desire. A cue activates that pattern in the brain, resulting in desire.

Now for some good news! When a particular pattern *doesn't* get reinforced, the cells begin to disconnect. The connections don't disappear instantly but they do become weaker and weaker when that particular pattern of brain cell signalling is no longer activated. This is the really important bit. In order for the cells to disconnect and the patterns to break down, *cells on both sides of the connection should be active.* For example, cells on one side of a connection could be about taking a coffee break. The cells on the other side are your desire to smoke. When you no longer satisfy your desire to smoke, the connection fades.

It's when the pattern in the brain is *activated and experienced* that these connections begin to weaken. When you are feeling your addictive desire – when you allow yourself to feel unsatisfied – those are the moments when real transformation takes place because those are the moments when you physically change the circuits in your brain. You are disconnecting 'coffee break' and 'have a cigarette' – *and you can only do that at the coffee break.* This is why avoiding the cues doesn't make much of a difference. This is why, when a cue is encountered for the first time, the addictive desire can be as strong as ever.

This might sound unusual but it is well established in some fields, especially in cognitive therapy for phobias and obsessive-compulsive disorders (OCD).[3] This therapy involves the same process of experiencing the established associations and choosing new responses. OCD is driven by the fear that something dreadful will happen if a particular ritual, such as handwashing, is not performed. This belief is challenged by not performing the ritual and discovering that it is in fact safe. For example, getting the hands 'dirty', having a strong desire to wash them, but not doing so. This activates the fear, breaks it down and actually makes an impact on the physical workings of the brain. Then the obsessive thoughts fade because they have nothing to reinforce them.

This process has been verified by 'before' and 'after' brain scans of people with OCD. Prior to therapy, the scans show a particular area of the brain with a much higher level of dopamine neurotransmitter activity than normal. The scans are completely normal after as little as two months of this kind of cognitive therapy.

Phobias and anxiety disorders are treated very successfully in the same way. No matter what a person is fearful of – birds, insects, being in lifts or public places – the way forward is for them to gradually expose themselves to the feared object or situation and slowly learn that they can be trusted. As they allow themselves to feel and accept this fear, it begins to lessen. In time, the patterns in the brain that connect fear to the feared object are weakened and the phobia fades.

In the field of addiction, this approach is called Cue Exposure Therapy, and it has been known for a long time that when the cues are experienced but not reinforced, the association fades. Cue Exposure Therapy, however, has not been widely used in the treatment of addiction because it hasn't produced particularly good results. There are a number of reasons for this, and it's going to be helpful for you to understand what they are. First, whenever people start to get interested in taking control of an addiction, most of them deny that they have got choices. This creates so much rebellion and miserable feelings of deprivation, it over-rides any benefit gained from breaking the connections. Just as important, though, is that the aim of Cue Exposure Therapy has usually been to completely eliminate all addictive desire, and in the vast majority of cases this is simply not possible.

Once particular patterns in the brain have been established, they can be allowed to fade but they don't disappear entirely. Some amount of addictive desire remains, even though it can be infrequent and very brief. Not only that, but it takes very little reinforcement to get the connections going again. If the addictive desire is satisfied, especially if it's done a few times, that pattern comes back into action very easily. It's really the same as having mastered things such as riding a bike, swimming or speaking a foreign language. Even when we don't use that skill for years, we can bring it back much more quickly than if we were starting from scratch.

This means that although you can greatly reduce the addictive desire by facing the cues and breaking the connections, you will also need to learn how to manage the level of desire that remains. Conveniently, you do both of these at the same time.

Managing Addictive Desire

Scientists used to believe that connections in the brain were formed very early in our life, during our very early years and even before birth.[4] They thought that the connections were permanent once they had been formed, but now we know it's not like that at all. Much of the research on this was pioneered by those involved in treating people with serious injury to the brain, either as a result of accidents or illness such as a stroke. Initially the brain injury has a bottom-up effect on the mind, severely impairing many of the thinking processes we take for granted. But the physical damage can be repaired and normal mental functioning restored. This is not achieved through surgery or pharmaceuticals, but through the power of the mind. The brain restores itself and rebuilds itself, and this process is aided by mental exercises.

Doctors who specialise in brain rehabilitation have found that when it comes to these mental exercises, just two qualities are required:

★ paying attention;
★ repetition.

So, when you pay attention to this process and when you are willing to repeat it, you get the lasting results you are after because you make a physical impact on your brain and how it works. This is how you get neurotransmitters to do what you want them to do. You just tell them, very clearly, over and over again!

What you pay attention to is your addictive desire, because that's when the cell patterns can disconnect.[5] Addictive desire is not the enemy and it's not even just a pain to be endured. *Addictive desire is the healing process itself.* When you experience it, that's when the changes in the brain take place. It needs to be managed correctly, but when you manage your feelings of addictive desire, that's when you use your willpower in the correct and most effective way. You have an impulse to act in one direction and you use the power of your will to act in another. After some repetition (not a lot, really) your new behaviour is established.

Managing addictive desire is important because it's not *just* exposure to the cues and desire that's necessary; what's critical is what you say to yourself at the time. When you manage your addictive desire correctly, you lessen the intensity and persistence of stronger cravings to a much more reasonable and acceptable level. And you cope with the level of addictive desire that remains – especially the familiar ways of thinking that support and justify it.

There are two key concepts to apply, and the first is one we have already covered in Chapter Three:

Own your choices

When you try to use willpower, if you think in terms of 'I must…I have to…I've got to…I can't…' you have the prohibitive attitude that belongs to slavery, and this exaggerates your craving, making it more intense and more persistent. This exaggeration is caused by your instinctual need to rebel against the restrictions you've imposed.

While you're trying hard to stay in control, your imagined loss of freedom can generate the feelings of deprivation, anger, sadness, self-pity – and even overwhelming cravings and obsession. Not only that, but you're likely to come up with any excuse you can find to cave in, at the same time losing sight of why you wanted to do such a silly thing as to use willpower in the first place. What a disaster!

Whenever you think you're not allowed to do something, you'll want it all the more and eventually act out being 'bad' and do it anyway! If you don't change that thinking you might follow the rules and manage to be 'good' for a while, but as we've already discussed, you'll find it tough to continue in the longer term. Slavery is not something that sits well with most of us.

Knowing you're free to choose is the only effective way to relate to your feelings of addictive desire. After all, people fight wars for freedom. If you don't feel free to do whatever you want to do, you'll be at war with yourself.

Even starting to develop a true sense of choice will make a dramatic impact on the top-down effect of mind on feelings of craving and deprivation. You'll be able to experience this for yourself when, instead of satisfying it, you start to choose to feel your addictive desire.

Thinking through addictive desire

Being addicted to something means that you've trained yourself not to control this one kind of impulse. So, whenever you experience your addictive desire, a particular way of thinking comes with it, all part of the same package. This way of thinking has also etched itself over time into the neural patterns in your brain, so it becomes automatic. This way of thinking puts you into an altered state of consciousness not unlike a kind of hypnotic trance. Even though you didn't deliberately set out to do this, it is self-induced. This is very helpful to know because if you created it, then you can create something different.

It is really nothing more than a belief system that you developed over time that automatically selects certain thoughts and disregards others. It cons you by presenting only one side of the picture. Addictive desire is sheer deception, often barely conscious, so that you're not even aware that this scam is going on. I expect, though, that you can see that there have been countless times in the past when you responded to your addictive desire, as you reached for another cigarette, or whatever, and:

Addictive Thinking

★ As much as you possibly could, you **denied** the negative consequences of this behaviour. The poor health, waste of money and lower self-esteem may at times flash through your mind in that moment of desire, but you habitually dismiss these thoughts as quickly as possible. To give these things attention while you are feeling your addictive desire puts you in an uncomfortable state of conflict, so they are better ignored.

★ For the same reason, you **emphasised** the positive aspects of what you were about to do, focusing on the pleasure you'd get, how helpful it would be and how it would enhance your life in some way.

★ You **justified** the addiction in a way that was appropriate to the circumstances you were in at the time. If you were busy, you needed to take a break. If you were relaxing you deserved a reward. If you were with others, you wanted to join in with the group. If you were on your own, you needed to cheer yourself up (or maybe it didn't matter because no one was looking!). There's no end to the number of justifications, and some may be unique to you.

★ You **resigned** yourself to the inevitability of satisfying this desire, with thoughts such as 'This is just the way I am', 'Everybody else is doing it', 'Everybody knows it's impossible to break this habit' or 'I'll stop one day.'

★ You took **action** by satisfying your addictive desire, and in doing so you strengthened the cue and this addictive thinking one more time.

Addictive thinking seems just like any other kind of thinking. Addictive thinking makes satisfying your addictive desire seem sensible and reasonable. Remember that we all have a built-in reward system that motivates us to support our life, and that an addiction hijacks this system, creating our attraction. This connects to a strong survival instinct that's programmed into us all. Even if the reward ('high' or 'buzz') is very occasional, and even if you're at the stage where it provides very little pleasure any more, a powerful association will have already been reinforced over many years between the behaviour and the reward. You may be more than ready to quit the addiction, but your 'gut feeling' of addictive desire is going to urge you to keep at it, producing the addictive thinking. This is why addictive desire can be mistaken for genuine need; why, for example, addictive hunger and natural hunger can be so easily confused.

You access willpower by challenging the addictive thinking at the time it's happening. You do this by paying attention to addictive desire, and:

Managing Desire

★ You **acknowledge** the addictive desire and name it for what it is: nothing more than your memory of past behaviour. As soon as you've done this you've broken the trance and started to create some distance from it.

★ You remind yourself you've got **free choices** about what you do. One choice you have is not to satisfy the addictive desire, and this will leave you feeling unsatisfied and uncomfortable. The other choice open to you is to satisfy it. It will help if you remember that this may leave you uncomfortable as well, perhaps less healthy in some way, out of control and having lower self-esteem. Using willpower is all about waking up to these choices.

★ You **challenge the justifications** and demonstrate to yourself that they don't hold water. You can only do that by taking control and going into situations and learning how to cope with them without the addictive behaviour. You'll find this is much more straightforward when you manage your feeling of addictive desire.

★ You **change your priorities**, by being willing to feel the addictive desire and not satisfy it. You decide that it's worth it to you to have the feeling of unsatisfied desire because it means you get your life back, it means you are in control.

★ You **relax** into the feeling of desire and **allow** it to be there, as much as you possibly can. The more you fear it, the more you resist it and wish it would go away, the worse it gets.

★ You deliberately recall your **motivation** to change by thinking of the ways your life will improve as a direct result of
feeling the desire instead of satisfying it. This is especially
effective while you're feeling the desire. You remind yourself that this feeling brings you specific improvements in
the quality of your life. Improvement in your self-esteem is
the most effective motivation to recall.

★ You **end your conflict** with your addictive desire. You make
your peace with it by seeing it as the way you change, the
way you exercise the power of your will.

This is not easy, especially at first, although it might not be as
difficult as it seems. It's certainly more difficult than simply
avoiding, ignoring and dismissing the desire – but it is exactly
where the magic happens, what changes everything.

If you avoid feeling your addictive desire, either through
pharmaceuticals or through keeping busy and changing your
routines, you don't break the connections in the brain and you
don't master the skill of managing addictive desire which is so
essential in the longer term. Then, when the addictive desire
returns, willpower disappears.

So it really depends on whether you want something that
works for a while but lets you down later on, or something
that's really going to last this time. Addictive desire only *causes*

addictive behaviour when it's not managed correctly. Most people miss the opportunity it presents; it's a healing feeling.

Why This Is the Best Way Out

There is a quote attributed to Helen Keller which says it all: 'The best way out is always through.' In case you don't know her story, an illness left Keller blind and deaf when she was just eighteen months old. Eventually, with a lot of help, she learned to write and speak, and went on to gain a degree, become a popular public speaker and write bestselling books, among numerous other achievements. I would suggest that her 'best way out is always through' philosophy is what made this possible.

Once you make that all-important shift to face and work through your experience of addictive desire, willpower is within your grasp. And so many other things fall into place behind it that this really does make it the best way out.

★ **You have a real choice** – when you allow yourself to feel the feeling of addictive desire. If you will not face and manage your addictive desire, you'll be compelled to satisfy it.

★ **You can succeed long term** – by accepting that there are limits to what the mind can do. For example, if you've had a leg amputated, you cannot think yourself a new one. In the same way, you cannot completely think away the scar in your brain that is your memory of past addictive behaviour. The cues and associations fade but they might not go away entirely. This unwelcome truth can put people off using willpower at all, so remember that the addictive desire fades away to almost nothing – provided it's handled correctly. In time, your addictive desire passes through your mind very occasionally, and very briefly. However, it's best to think carefully when it's there.[6]

★ **You can take control** – when you are willing to look addictive desire in the face. If you fear your feeling of addictive desire, you'll probably try to ignore it. When you are in the habit of ignoring it, you can automatically feed it without even realising what you're doing. The more you deal with your desire consciously, the less likely this is to happen.

★ **You can separate your addictions and/or habits** – by dealing with one at a time. This is especially helpful if you want to take control of only one type of behaviour, because you're not ready to change everything in your life all at once, and you might not want to, ever. Not only do you not need to do this, but it's best if you tackle just one challenge with willpower at a time. For example, there are smokers who want to stop smoking tobacco but want to continue to smoke cannabis. Smoking dope will trigger an addictive desire for tobacco if the association between them has been made, which is often the case. Facing and managing the addictive desire to smoke tobacco means it will eventually fade. Then you are left with the remaining habit, which may or may not be an addiction and may or may not be some-thing you want to quit. Other examples might be overeating and watching TV, drinking alcohol and smoking, playing video games and drinking cola.

★ **You can keep some control over other addictions and/or habits** – When people don't manage their addictive desire for one substance, they usually end up satisfying it with another. This is why a smoker might overeat when they quit – and an overeater might increase their smoking when they diet! They are trying to recreate the buzz with something else. When desire for one substance is managed correctly, other behaviours and addictions stay the same.

★ **You don't need to rearrange your life** – In fact, it's best to carry on as usual, meet cues as they happen and practise the skill of dealing with them. This is exactly when and where you practise using your willpower.

★ **You don't necessarily need to examine your emotions** – in order to use willpower. Some people, especially addictive overeaters, go into therapy for years hoping to get rid of their addictive desire. They are often told that they are trying to fill an emotional void with food, with the implication that excess weight is evidence that there's some-thing 'wrong' with them. When they discover the upsetting experience that started it all, heal that past trauma or forgive that parent who let them down, they will no longer need to overeat. This can play a part in some cases, but it is by no means relevant all the time. There are too many examples of people who've got their emotional lives and relationships as sorted out as anyone else, and all they need to do is start to pay attention to addictive desire. You are not mad or bad for having the desire. You simply did something addictive in the past and you now have a memory of that.

Breaking Dependency

I remember talking on the phone with a client who had quit smoking six months earlier, and I was asking, as usual, how he was coping with his addictive desire. It didn't come often, he told me, and was very brief but sometimes very surprising. Just last week he was simply sitting on a park bench with the sun on his face, relaxed and content, and suddenly he wanted to smoke. He managed that desire with no problem but was curious about why it happened. When we talked further we realised that, as he had quit in the autumn and now it was spring, this was the first time he had sat on a park bench with the sun on his face. He had done this in the past while smoking, probably on that same bench. The first time a cue is met it's stronger, because those memory connections have not yet broken down.

The tragedy about this is that often people take control of addiction for a while without encountering certain cues, either because they're deliberately avoiding them or because the situations just don't happen all that often. They make lots of good changes, taking control of their overeating for example, and do very well for a period of time. Then, perhaps weeks later, they encounter a particular situation for the first time and they fall back into overeating again. The last time they were in this situation they overate, so there's suddenly a stronger connection, a sense of desire that has yet to fade.

If they don't know how to manage their addictive desire, they usually satisfy it at these times, perhaps even unconsciously and automatically. Then they blame the circumstance for the relapse. People think they were doing fine until they got stressed at work, until they went on holiday, until they spent an evening alone or until they had a fight with their husband. Then, it seems that situation caused their relapse. This is why people believe they are dependent on their addictions. You break your dependency by dealing with your addictive desire in those particular circumstances, discovering that you don't need the addiction at all.

When you know about the cues and connections in the brain, you can see things in a different light. All of these situations present nothing other than more brain connections to be rerouted. They are memories that can be allowed to fade.

Without this information you can get all fired up to change your ways but totally lose the plot when you experience that desire.

What makes the difference is to develop the skill of recognising and managing the addictive desire, which is the impulse or craving you feel. Understand that you make it far more acceptable when you practise dealing with it correctly. And remember that not only can the desire be tolerated, but it is the healing process itself.

In an addiction we have one of the most extraordinary examples of mind–body teamwork. The experience of desire is rooted in biochemistry. The reaction to it, which makes up the real difficulty – the drama, the rebelliousness, the loss of control, the excuses and justifications – is controllable by the mind. Both interact together. The mind can harm by creating obstacles to recovery. Or it can heal – making willpower a joy to use.

Strengthening Choice

The correct use of willpower weakens the reward patterns in the brain, but at the same time there is another part of the brain that gets strengthened. This is the area where choices are made. The location of our ability to choose has been identified through experiments using brain scanning technology.

In one experiment, volunteers lay in a PET scan doing nothing more than lifting a finger, while researchers studied the parts of the brain that were activated.[7] First they told the volunteers which finger to move and when to move it. Then they let them decide themselves. There was a very clear difference between the two. As soon as the subjects started to make their own decisions, an area of the brain sprang into life which had previously been inactive. The action of moving a finger was the same in both instances. The difference was in choosing it rather than following orders.

This activity was in the prefrontal cortex, in a region which lies just behind the forehead. It's *the most adaptable part of the brain* and it's the part that's the most highly evolved. It's the part of our brain that is proportionally far larger than in any other animal, and it gives us our most human qualities. This is where our self-awareness lies, and our ability to choose for ourselves.

When you practise owning choices, as introduced in Chapter Three, and when you continue to think in terms of your own choice, you will be strengthening that part of your brain, just as the taxi drivers developed part of their brains.

If, for example, you follow a diet as if you're following orders, you won't be thinking in terms of choice and you won't develop that area of your brain. And as a result, the problems from feeling deprived never improve. On the other hand, when you start to own choice (even while you're making choices you regret, although it will be more effective to choose the unsatisfied desire) you'll strengthen your choice-making muscles and thinking in terms of choice will come more naturally to you.

If this all sounds a bit daunting, remember that the ways you think already have an effect on the way your brain works – whether you like it or not! The question is whether or not you want to make changes or follow the same patterns as before. You either strengthen particular patterns in your brain or you weaken them – all the time, every day. If you just get ever so slightly better at rewiring the connections, you'll do fine. Some perseverance will be needed, and this is what we'll look at next.

Step by Step

★ **Don't wait it out, passively** – Since the difficulties are created in large part by the mind, they can only be resolved by a shift in thinking. Waiting for these feelings to go away means you are still thinking in terms of a purely physical process of recovery. Use your mind and you'll go much further much faster. Use your mind and using willpower will be a positive, rewarding and effective experience.

★ **Break the trance state of desire** – At first, it can be a struggle to change your thinking. Start out by paying attention to moments of addictive desire and name them for what they are. If you don't deliberately intervene, the old patterns of thinking will follow by default. It takes conscious effort and a deliberate intention to change this.

★ **Allow yourself to feel your addictive desire** – Your feeling of addictive desire is your opportunity to change. This is when you change the patterns of connections in your brain and when you work through it, learning to spot addictive thinking and manage the desire. The more you do this when you start out, the more likely you'll be able to stay in control in times of crisis and upset.

★ **Watch out for cues that are thoughts and emotions** – as well as situations and circumstances. If I eat something every time I feel bored, thinking I'm bored will trigger my addictive desire to eat. If I stop off at the corner shop to buy a huge tub of ice cream whenever I come home from work feeling unappreciated, having a bad day at work is my cue for this addictive desire.

★ **Start to let go of your fear and your resistance to feeling this desire** – Resistance to the addictive desire is usually the fear that it will overwhelm you. You think it's wrong to have these feelings and if you were doing it 'right' you wouldn't have any addictive desire. If you hang on to the idea that the desire will go away or should go away, you won't be coming to terms with it, and in fact you make it worse. More about this in our next chapter.

★ **Give yourself permission to continue the addiction in order to fully own choice** – This may be a tough step to take, but you can only feel truly free when you know that you could spend the rest of your life smoking, overeating, gambling or whatever. From there, you can begin to make different choices – assuming that's what you want to do! While you deny these choices you'll find it tough to get started.

★ **Choose the feeling of desire** – If you think of choosing 'not to smoke' or 'not to overeat' you may still be ignoring the addictive desire, so it's much better to think of choosing 'to accept the feeling of desire'.

★ **See through your own defence systems and denial** – See if you find it easier to acknowledge the health hazards of addictions you *don't* have. For example, if you don't consume sugar-free items, you might be happy to accept that the artificial sweetener aspartame is quite toxic. Those who don't smoke can easily see the damage smoking causes. Another way to see through denial is to ask yourself if you'd want your children, or others you love, to do what you're doing.

★ **Learn about nutrition** – If you follow the common advice to 'give your body whatever it wants' you'll simply be reinforcing the same patterns in the brain with the same behaviour. These patterns are likely to be strongest in connection with those foods that have the most addictive quality to them. As you might expect, these are the foods that are bad for your health. Not only do they not contain the nutrition you need, but they contain an anti-nutritional content, which means they make you ill. As far as your health is concerned, you would be better off if you didn't eat them at all. Excess weight is often a sign of being undernourished. It's a dangerous myth that if you eat poorly, eventually your body will tell you it needs proper food and you'll find yourself craving vegetables. This is simply not the case.

★ **Re-educate your taste buds** – For many overeaters, willpower is much easier to use with food that doesn't contain sugar, wheat, fats or salt. Some say they don't enjoy natural foods, such as fruit and vegetables, that have no addictive ingredients. This is because they have become so used to satisfying addictive desire, eating in a way that isn't addictive seems unsatisfying. More natural foods are easier to control, though, and in time you will find them more appealing.

★ **Give up the idea that you're too old to make changes** – This is only true if you want it to be. Your brain is always growing, making new connections. It slows down a bit as you get older – but it never stops!

Where There's a Will: Deborah

I smoked for eighteen years and I have been an ex-smoker for eight, yet I still feel the desire to smoke. Usually the experience is very mild nowadays but up until only a couple of years ago

I was amazed by how intense, even if brief, the desire could be. The intensity of it makes me understand how, even after years of stopping, some people can take a cigarette if offered one at one of those overwhelmingly desirous moments. You would be caught completely unawares if you didn't understand the nature of addictive desire.

I smoked forty-plus cigarettes a day and proudly hung on to the fact that I had read that women become pharmacologically addicted to cigarettes if they smoke more than twenty a day. It wasn't my fault! I was addicted! Whenever I gave up – and I did it cold turkey, with hypnosis, with acupuncture, with nicotine gum – I would feel desperate and almost literally suicidal. Certainly life no longer felt worth living. I expected three days of utter misery – and tried to minimise them by sleeping through large portions of them – but inevitably my misery worsened after three days instead of lessening. I have either given in at six days or at best struggled through four months of non-living. Friends used to say it was as if I wasn't really there, and that was true. I was always just getting through time, waiting for oblivion.

The common advice to avoid triggers always seemed a nonsense to me. Yes, you can give up tea or coffee and not visit pubs for a while, but how can you live any kind of normal life at all if one of your triggers for smoking is the act of getting up in the morning, and your usual pattern is to have a cigarette with every possible activity, including after a bath, after sex, while working, walking and immediately before sleeping.

This nonsense made me relate at once to the idea of experiencing your addictive desire instead of trying to avoid it. (I had also tried to avoid it by excessive exercise or alcohol.) The important thing was that I was choosing to feel the temporary discomfort of the desire rather than have the more permanent accompanying discomforts of being a smoker. I wasn't resentful, I wasn't blaming anyone else for making me not smoke, I was taking responsibility for myself.

When I stopped this time I ate and drank no more and no less than I did as a smoker and did not put on any weight. I did not get irritable and it made no difference to me whether I was with smokers or non-smokers. I am not saying that stopping smoking was easy, but to all intents and purposes my life went on as before and no one would have known I had quit.

Notes

1. 'The posterior hippocampi of taxi drivers were significantly larger relative to those of control subjects (who did not drive taxis). Hippocampal volume correlated with the amount of time spent as a taxi driver. It seems that there is a capacity for local plastic change in the structure of the healthy adult human brain in response to environmental demands.' Published in *Proceedings of the National Academy of Sciences* (2000) 11;97(8):4398–4403.

2. This is from *A User's Guide to the Brain* by John J. Ratey, MD, Associate Clinical Professor of Psychiatry at Harvard Medical School: 'The lesson here is that we have the power to change our brains. The human brain's amazing plasticity enables it to continually rewire and learn, not just through academic study but through experience, thought, action, and emotion.'

And from Dr Herbert Benson in his book *Timeless Healing* (Simon & Schuster, 1996): 'It is possible to mobilize our thoughts to change the way our brains work, to shape our nerve cells with experiences and events that are emotionally fulfilling and not emotionally threatening…'

3. This is from *A User's Guide to the Brain*, referring to overcoming a phobia of heights: 'The flooding process is straight cognitive behavioural training; it is rearranging the circuits in the brain, reducing all the neural connections that have long supported the thesis that height equals falling while strengthening the circuits that convey "safe". By gradually rewiring, the patient begins to refocus on the fact that he's not going to fall off the building.'

Jerilyn Ross, MA, President of the Anxiety Disorders Association of America, writes in her book *Triumph Over Fear*: 'Scientists now know that drugs can influence neurotransmitters. They also know that psychological therapies can have the same influence, although they may take longer…[Going] through the situations that induce the most anxious feelings can actually change the chemistry of the brain in powerful, long-lasting, curative ways.'

Changes in brain activity following cognitive therapy have also been seen in scans of patients with schizophrenia. In comparison with a control group, 'the patient group that received successful Cognitive Remediation Therapy had significantly increased brain activation in regions associated with working memory'. This report, 'Effects on the brain of a psychological treatment', was published in the *British Journal of Psychiatry* (2002),181;144–152.

4. This is from *Mind Sculpture* by Dr Ian Robertson, one of the world's leading researchers on brain rehabilitation and Professor of Psychology at Trinity College, Dublin: 'It is often argued that the brain is 'hard-wired', meaning that if the wiring is broken, then change is impossible. It is true that the brain is hard-wired to a great extent, but research over the last ten years has proved dramatically that in fact its wiring can be much less 'hard' than was once thought.' And: '...my research group showed that how well people can pay attention just after a right-brain stroke predicts how well they can use their left hands two years later!' This report published in *Neuropsychology* (1997),11;290–295.

5. This is from Jerilyn Ross' book *Triumph Over Fear*, which explains a very similar process for those with obsessive-compulsive disorder: 'That means exposing yourself every day to the very things that make you uncomfortable. And it means stopping yourself from doing the things that reassure you.'

6. One study has been able to demonstrate that when thoughts of desire are ignored, 'the very behaviour one was trying to prevent becomes increasingly likely to occur.' *International Journal of Eating Disorders* (26;21-27, 1999) 'Suppressing Thoughts about Chocolate'.

7. 'Willed action and the prefrontal cortex in man', *Proceedings of the Royal Society of London: Biological Sciences* (1991), 22; 244:241–246.

CHAPTER SEVEN

The Will to Persevere

The changes in attitude that bring lasting success

It's often said that those who succeed in something aren't necessarily the most talented but are simply those who have persisted the longest. Unfortunately, the need to persevere puts many people off using willpower at all. Yet most things in life are only there because you maintain them. The list is endless: personal hygiene, a job or career, a clean house, relationships, a nice garden, rent or mortgage payments. You wouldn't even be alive unless you persevered with fairly regular supplies of food, water, air and sleep. The question is not whether we need to persevere with willpower. Of course we do. It is whether or not perseverance is a struggle which takes an unreasonable amount of effort and never eases up.

Often, when people think about persevering, they think

about keeping going with a struggle. That's why it seems so gloomy and so doomed to failure. When perseverance is like treading water, just trying not to drown, it's more likely to wear you down sooner or later.

The change in attitude is not to pretend you don't need to persevere but to see it in a more optimistic light. Perseverance needs to be about getting somewhere, about making progress. You make progress by starting to think in new ways and making these ways of thinking your own. Then there's much less effort because the new thinking is natural to you, so it's much easier to follow. This chapter is about making those changes.

Changing Your Mind

Changing your thinking means being willing to let go of familiar thoughts and beliefs, the attitudes and opinions you may have held for many years. As you probably know, it can often be easier said than done.

Some people get stuck because they rely too much on what they regard as gut feelings or intuition. These feelings seem to express who they are, their identity, which makes it tough even to begin to see that things could be any different. But feelings, even strong and familiar feelings, aren't necessarily the best indication of what actions to take. Feelings can simply be the result of out-of-date ways of thinking. They can come from attitudes that really don't fit the present circumstances. They can even come from believing things that simply aren't true.

To illustrate this point, I could make a mistake with the numbers and *think* I've won the lottery. I'll *feel* undeniable feelings of joy and excitement, and if I follow my feelings I'm likely to go out and spend huge amounts of money. Doing what your feelings tell you to do can lead to disaster. I'm not suggesting you disregard your feelings entirely, simply that you use your head as well as your heart to guide you. Just because you feel like overeating or smoking doesn't necessarily mean it would be wise to act on that. Just because you don't feel motivated to use willpower doesn't mean you would do best to value that feeling.

Feelings are fickle, especially when it comes to addiction. Just about anybody with an addiction in their lives can relate to how much and how often their feelings about it change. You can be consumed with regret and guilt after a binge, but it's unlikely these feelings will surface at all in a moment of addictive desire. This is the nature of addiction.

It's very easy for us to assume our habitual thoughts are accurate and that the feelings associated with them are valuable, but this is not necessarily the case. If we don't challenge these thoughts and feelings, we will assume they are correct, and feel and act as if they are. When it comes to addiction there are three central belief systems to challenge, and when you do this, the difficult feelings associated with these beliefs fade.

Challenging False Beliefs

★ **FALSE: Willpower limits your freedom of choice** – As you begin to challenge this by owning choice, the feelings of deprivation, self-pity, sadness and anger will disappear. And because you don't need to rebel when you have total freedom, the intense cravings, obsession and justifications fade as well.

★ **FALSE: Addictive desire is the enemy** – Fighting and resenting the feeling of addictive desire makes it worse, and the desire isn't nearly so much of a problem as is your resistance to it. As you overcome your resistance and start to face, feel and manage your addictive desire, feelings of fear and anxiety will fade and the desire will diminish as well.

★ **FALSE: Addiction supports and enhances your life[1]** – This belief creates your sense of dependency, the fear that you won't be able to cope with your life or enjoy yourself as much, without the addiction. If you manage your addictive desire correctly, as you begin to take control you'll begin to see through these beliefs. You will find that you cope better when you have stronger willpower and feel considerably happier when you have stronger self-esteem, so the anxiety about being dependent disappears.

These three beliefs make up the addictive thinking that supports addiction. This addictive belief system acts as a filter, and everything – including any information and your own experiences – gets filtered and understood via the addictive thinking. Within the addictive belief system, the satisfaction of addictive desire is the priority, so anything that throws that into question is itself questioned or disregarded as much as possible. And any idea that supports the satisfaction of addictive desire will be valued.

First, see that these are just thoughts in the first place. They are persistent but they aren't cast in stone. The point is, you can change your thoughts, with some persistence. At the very least open yourself up to the possibility of change. A good first step is to recognise that maybe you're not completely right about something. Maybe there's another way of looking at things, even though you're not able to see what this is yet.

I once heard of an experiment that was carried out many years ago at a university which demonstrated how tough it can be for us to admit we're wrong about something. It was a version of the old rats-in-a-maze experiment. There's a maze of corridors, with walls tall enough so the rats can't see over them. A piece of cheese is placed at some point in the maze and the rats are studied to see how long it takes them to find the cheese and whether they remember where it is the next day. When the cheese gets moved, it's noted how quickly the rats can change their route to discover the new location in the maze.

In the experiment I heard about, the maze was made large

enough so that rats could be replaced by human volunteers. The cheese was replaced by money. When the results were compared between the rats and the people it was found that there was a huge difference between them. Once they had discovered the location of their reward, the human rats found it much more difficult to change, trying the same corridors over and over again, long after the reward was relocated. I can imagine them saying to themselves, 'I know it's down here…I just know it…it was here yesterday…it must be here!'

Unlike rats, we can observe our thoughts and observe ourselves observing. We can deliberately choose our thoughts and change our thinking. But our incredibly complicated brains mean that we can also stubbornly hold on to what we 'know' is right. Maybe it's time to look down another corridor, even though you *know* it's the wrong one!

Your beliefs look accurate to you, and this is exactly why changing your thinking is a challenge. You start out in the face of evidence to the contrary. For example, all your evidence may point to the fact that your life will fall apart if you stop smoking. All your evidence may be that you will never succeed in taking control of overeating. All your evidence may be that any use of willpower leaves you vulnerable, depressed and doomed to fail. What is required is to be willing to say that *maybe* it isn't so.

If you aren't willing to question these beliefs, perseverance continues to be a struggle. The good part about this is that if you just start to change a few bits here and there, you will see and feel positive results which will give you good feedback that you're on the right track. Making progress in changing these beliefs has a circular nature: as you progress, you make progress easier.

The flip side of this is a vicious circle: the more you fail, the more convinced you are that you'll fail and the more likely you are to fail.

Breaking Through Vicious Circles

Vicious circles hold you down, they are the negative, self-defeating beliefs that keep you stuck in your addictive behaviours. They appear as lines of thinking that sound something like this: 'I'll never be good at that...see, I did it wrong...I knew I would...I won't bother to try any more.'

In other words you predict failure, make an attempt, meet an obstacle and resign yourself to failure. A vicious circle fuels itself, reinforcing all those doubts in your ability to change, strengthening your sense of helplessness. These negative circles can continue for years. They can seem to be who we are, how we think of ourselves, how we define ourselves: maybe not too bad at some things but completely useless at willpower, especially in particular areas.

You begin to make real progress when you begin to challenge and break out of these vicious circles. This will sound something like: 'I'll try that even though it seems scary...I sort of did it although not perfectly...I've never managed anything like that before...maybe I could learn from my mistakes and figure out how to do it better.'

It will take time to make these positive circles a real part of your thinking, but with persistence you will begin to achieve the results you are after. The key to moving from a negative circle towards a positive one is to find out what it is that can break any particular vicious circle for you. You could start with 'stepping stones' that aren't connected with your main goal, but it's good to find the right ones for you. They are going to be different for everybody because one person's mountain to climb is another person's walk in the park. That doesn't matter in the slightest – just look for whatever could be your next step. With any success you achieve you begin to turn around those deep-seated beliefs about not having willpower. This only happens, though, provided you (privately and deliberately) acknowledge your successes along the way.

As you proceed you may come up against convictions that you were just born with no willpower, or that it was the way you were raised, or it's your genes that make you this way and that nothing will ever change. Just making one change – provided it presents a reasonable degree of challenge – starts to break down this belief system. Once you've begun this process you can see that change is possible and you develop even the smallest sense of hope for the future.

These circles are important to understand because, as you'll see when you begin to notice them, they will either drag you down into low moods, apathy and low self-esteem or pull you up into hopefulness, optimism and stronger self-esteem. When you invite hope back into your life – no matter what your current circumstances are – you get in touch with all kinds of possibilities. Those possibilities could be frighteningly exciting (!), so take things one step at a time.

Simply start to become aware of what's happening when you're in the grip of a vicious circle. Just one challenge begins to move you from the negative to the positive. As the next step in your life appears, you choose a new response. Will it be helpless or powerful?

Here are some thoughts about vicious circles for five of the themes we've looked at already. These are the circular patterns of belief that generate behaviour…that reinforce beliefs…that generate behaviour…and so on.

Self-esteem

The vicious circle is in believing that you're not worth taking care of…so you have no motivation to make changes…so you don't use willpower to make changes…which proves you're not worth the bother. If you can see that you have strong willpower when it comes to doing things for others, but not so much when taking care of yourself, it will be clear to you that this is an issue of self-esteem. This isn't the case with everybody but it's certainly very common.

In breaking out of this circle, the two most useful things to remember are that self-esteem is always a matter of degree, and that it's always completely in your hands. Many people make the mistake of thinking about self-esteem in 'all or none' terms: either they have it or they don't. When you realise it's a matter of degree, raising your self-esteem becomes possible.

When you see what a difference it makes even to raise your self-esteem a little, and when you understand that it can become stronger in time, you will have access to the most powerful and effective motivation there is. Your self-esteem is such a significant factor in your life, in what you do, how you feel, and how you relate to others, it will make a big difference, every now and then, to stop and consider it.

The key here is in knowing what higher self-esteem feels like, and, most importantly, what you need to do to create it. You'll miss out on this if you think you just went through a more productive phase of your life, or that you just happened to be in a good mood one day. You'll miss out if you think it was because a particular planet moved into or out of your star sign. If you can connect these positive states to sources of self-esteem, you'll have strong motivation to continue. And if you realise that they don't happen to you arbitrarily, you'll have a far greater degree of control over them.

Almost everybody could benefit from this awareness. Any form of addiction, including 'consumerism', relies on low levels of self-esteem. The premise behind most advertising is that if you buy the product you'll feel better about yourself and be more acceptable to others – and our whole culture buys into this myth. Yet record levels of depression and addiction are the tip-off that it simply doesn't work. The new product merely delivers a temporary illusion of self-esteem, reinforcing low self-esteem in the process.

You break out of this vicious circle when you begin to support your genuine self-esteem.[2] This, as we saw in Chapter Two, supports your willpower. The positive circle is completed by willpower further strengthening self-esteem.

Fear of freedom

Vicious circles run on fear, the circle being that your fear about something can make it come true. For example, when public speakers are very fearful of performing badly, that fear makes them perform badly. Which, in turn, makes them even more fearful.

With willpower, many people fear their freedom to choose. They fear, for example, that if they really are free to eat as much as they want, they will. So they deny free choice because it looks safer. But, as we saw in Chapter Three, denying free choice creates rebellion, so they do in fact end up overeating. The vicious circle continues when the binge ends and they start to drill into themselves that they *must never* do that again, and that they've *got to* change their ways. And so on.

The amount of fear that keeps this going is not overwhelming, though, and you can push through it with just a bit of effort. The more you practise choosing willpower, the more you'll be able to trust yourself to make the choices that are right for you. And the more you trust yourself, the less you'll fear your free choices.

Fear of addictive desire

Fear also gets in the way of managing addictive desire. The fear, of course, is that the desire will overwhelm you and send you out of control despite your best intentions. Whenever you're afraid of something your first reaction is to avoid it, and the most reliable way to avoid an addictive desire is to keep satisfying it – which confirms the fear! This is why so many people don't get started on using willpower in the first place or cave in at the first sign of temptation.

It's helpful to see that there are two different things here: your feeling of addictive desire and your fear of having that feeling. It's inevitable that you'll feel addictive desire, but if you fear it, this makes it much worse. The more you fight your addictive desire, the more it will seem to have power over you. The more you try to make it go away, the stronger and more dramatic it becomes. The more you resent it, the more likely you'll feel anxious at any hint of it appearing. This is very helpful to understand: it's not the feeling of addictive desire that creates the problems, it's your fear of it.

The key is to move forward into precisely what it is you are afraid of. This is exactly what I did when I overcame my fear of public speaking. The more you face the fear, the more it fades. When you can reassure yourself that your addictive desire is a safe feeling to have, you'll be able to manage it much better. And it's only going to feel safe when you can begin to trust yourself not to satisfy it.

You build this positive circle by gaining acceptance of these feelings of desire. The more you accept them, the easier they will become, the less anxious and tense you feel and the less you fear they will overpower you. This, in turn, makes the addictive desire much more acceptable.

You may have experienced this principle of acceptance if you have ever had to endure any degree of physical pain for any length of time. The natural inclination, of course, is to tense up and fight it, but when you counteract that, the pain lessens. You may have found out for yourself that when you stopped resisting it and allowed yourself to relax a bit, the pain subsided.

Motivation

Fear of failure can block your motivation to make changes so that you don't even want to bother in the first place. This is because, if you really let yourself want this new life that willpower could bring you, the more it will matter to you if you don't achieve it. Wanting very much to take control – while at the same time believing it's impossible – sets up a painful state of guilt and despair, so staying uncertain about making changes makes things feel a lot safer. And so, usually over many years, a numb state of resignation sets in. To feel enthusiastic about using willpower is too risky, so you train yourself not to feel it.

If you find it tough to identify particular goals, know that fear is getting in your way – fear of failure, maybe, or of commitment, of change itself or of losing control. Fear means that this is going to take some courage, not massive amounts, but enough so that you'll need to push yourself just a bit. Using willpower isn't like falling off a log.

It may be helpful to keep in mind that continuing the addiction is something you are increasingly likely to fear as well. As health, financial or relationship problems become more pressing, fear of these consequences tends to escalate. This can create another vicious circle because it increases your fear of failure when so much is riding on your success. This is why the sooner you start to use willpower the better. All you need to do is simply to take this into account as you set your sights on your willpower goals. With any success you achieve, you begin to break this vicious circle because you see that success is possible, that it really does bring you joy and that this is a joy you can keep for good.

Willpower

Most people hold beliefs about themselves that limit them, and as far as willpower is concerned, this is usually that they don't have any or don't have any in certain circumstances. For example, a person may believe that they don't have any willpower when they're out with friends. They tell themselves they're good at self-control when they're on their own, or while at work, but completely useless in social situations. Just like the other vicious circles we've been looking at, acting along these lines reinforces the belief, which encourages you to act along these lines…and so on.

A belief such as this may, to begin with, have been based on one or two experiences. It then gets reinforced so often that you may have no experience at all of it not being the case. A belief such as this can lead you to fail because it immediately undermines you. For example, you're offered a plate of biscuits. You'd prefer not to eat them but your first thought is that you don't have any willpower. So, acting on that thought, you eat the biscuits and in doing so you reinforce the belief: 'See, I knew I didn't have any willpower! I never do with biscuits!'

The difficulty in challenging this is that the belief looks real. One way to change it is first of all to choose it. Let yourself know: 'I choose to be someone who has no self-control with biscuits.' By owning the fact that you are the one who is holding this belief, you can start to get some power over it. When you choose it, then you can see that you could choose something else if you wanted to. You could manage your addictive desire instead.

The more you manage your addictive desire, the more you expect not to be satisfying it. One success with willpower gives you more confidence to use willpower in other areas of your life. Your new lifestyle becomes normal and natural to you; it simply becomes what you assume you will do. This new expectation provides you with a very powerful boost to your ability to persevere.

Change Your Expectations

The principle here is very simple. The less you expect to satisfy your addictive desire the less you'll feel it. The way you do this is to become as sure as you can that you prefer to use willpower. If you remain unsure, that uncertainty keeps your addictive desire more alive, more powerful and active. So, become as clear as you can as soon as you can about how you really want your life to be. If you can feel sure, this makes things easier and it means you're more likely to succeed.

A number of studies have demonstrated this point very clearly.[3] In brief, volunteer smokers were presented with different situations on two different days. On one day, the smokers found themselves in a situation that was clearly a smoking area and so they expected to be smoking. On the other day, the smokers were in a no-smoking area, so there was the expectation that they wouldn't smoke. Questionnaires were completed to evaluate how strongly the smokers wanted to smoke in each situation and there was a clear difference. They had much stronger cravings when they were in the smoking area. One of these studies concludes: 'It might be more fruitful to increase a sense of control by showing that behaviour is not triggered by an uncontrollable urge but to a large extent is the result of personal (self-fulfilling) expectancies.'

This matches the experience that many smokers have of these two kinds of situations in their lives. Smokers go into no-smoking areas – a plane, their doctor's surgery, a cinema or someone's office – knowing ahead of time that they're not going to be smoking while they are there. Even heavy long-term smokers find these situations manageable and often don't even experience their desire to smoke until they leave – which is when they expect to smoke.

I met one very heavy smoker not long ago who told me of

the time she flew from London to Australia and didn't experience any problems at all – no withdrawal symptoms, no craving, no irritability – during the twenty-four-hour flight. She knew when she booked that it was a non-smoking flight, and so she had no expectation at all of smoking on the plane. However, when she landed in Brisbane to change planes, she had expected to smoke at least one cigarette between flights. This was not permitted and that was when she got upset. Really upset.

There is also the fascinating example of American GIs who became hooked on heroin while fighting in Vietnam.[4] It was estimated that half of the soldiers became addicted during that war, using the drug almost daily for years, but only a tiny minority continued to use it on their return home. Not only did most of them break their addiction, but they did so effortlessly, with none of the usual notorious symptoms of withdrawal. This was partly because there were few cues associated with their addiction, but also because they had absolutely no expectation of drug use once they were home.

In order to make use of this concept, you take a long, hard look at what you want to value. What is worth more to you: satisfying your addictive desire, or managing that desire in order to gain control? You need to decide which of these you prefer – and nobody can ever decide that for you. Part of your evaluation will depend on how intensely and how often you feel your addictive desire, so it helps to reduce that to some extent. On the other hand, there are the benefits you get from being in control, so it helps to know what these benefits are.

The paradox is that the more sure you are that you'd rather feel and manage your addictive desire, the more it fades into the background. When you value the feeling of addictive desire because it brings you control, freedom, health, self-esteem and all the rest, this, finally, begins to lay it to rest.

Some ambivalence about this can be expected at first and it's inevitable that sometimes you'll automatically expect to satisfy your desire. For example, bread is delivered to your table at your favourite restaurant. You always eat it immediately, so you automatically have the expectation of doing that and you have the desire. You still don't have to act on that desire, though. You could manage it instead. You'll find that if you feel sure that you prefer not to satisfy it, it evaporates. It will return in the future, but the more convinced you can be that these things are not what you want to be doing, in general, the less desire for them you'll feel.

Being convinced about this, even while you feel your addictive desire, is something that takes a bit of time for most people. There are people who manage this degree of certainty from the moment they quit smoking or go on a diet. This is why some smokers and overeaters can make that decision and never feel tempted again. It's possible for a few people, and it does make things very easy – but don't count on it. It's something to aim towards. If this is very tough for you to do, though, it could be because you are forgetting that you have a choice.

If you find it absolutely impossible to become single-minded about your goals, your block may be that it seems to limit your free choice. Your ambivalence keeps you free from commitment, so it's important to stay ambivalent so that you feel free to choose either way. It will help to sort this out. Realise that it's entirely possible to be sure how you want to live your life and still know you've got the freedom to do otherwise. You can be sure you don't want to live your life smoking. You can be sure you want to have some control over what and how much you eat. You can be sure you want the best possible health and to live in a way that supports your self-esteem, to honour and respect yourself. You'll be much more able to stay in sight of these goals if you accept that you've still got the freedom to return to your old ways.

Changing these sorts of expectations is a very powerful thing to do and is an example of what I mean by making progress. When you start to change your thinking in this way, you change your priorities. It can come down to: what's more important to me, that cigarette or my self-esteem? When you *know* the answer is self-esteem – even while you're feeling your desire to smoke – perseverance will be effortless.

Failure and Perfectionism

Total failure and absolute perfection are at extreme ends of a scale, and identifying too closely with either one can create problems. If you are absolutely convinced of failure, you're not likely to try in the first place. At the other extreme, perfection can be tough to maintain, so it too can lead to hopelessness. The way through is to steer a path between the two.

The path you steer very much depends on what addiction you are wanting to control. It also depends on you and the extent to which you are addicted.

Smoking

Of all addictions, the one that is best handled in a perfect way is smoking. The vast majority of smokers either quit completely or they smoke all day, every day. One cigarette leads to another, so choosing to smoke after quitting usually means choosing to return to daily smoking.

In theory, you could use willpower to keep your smoking under control, but in practice this is virtually impossible to carry out. Some use this as evidence of physical dependency, but in fact it has much more to do with how you make choices. If you think your choices are between accepting the desire and smoking just one cigarette, the desire wouldn't seem preferable. It's only when you weigh up your choice between accepting the desire and the possibility of smoking every day for the rest of your life that managing the desire begins to look more attractive. Once you've smoked one cigarette, there's very little reason not to smoke another.

The best way to think about it is in terms of risk.[5] Smoking one cigarette means there's at least a *risk* you'll continue to smoke every day. Some fairly extensive research indicates that with one 'slip-up' 85 per cent of smokers return to full-time smoking. Knowing the risk you're taking may be the only thing that gets you to think twice, to break out of the trance of desire *before* you smoke that first cigarette.

Overeating

The addiction you would do well to handle in a not-so-perfect way is overeating, and perfectionism can be much more of a problem in using willpower with food. Overeaters who try to eat in a perfect way usually have a tendency towards perfectionism in other areas of their life. No matter what they achieve, they always think they should have done better.

With food, they are either perfectly in control or completely out of control, creating the highs and lows of dieting and bingeing. Perfectionism means it's all or nothing, so as soon as they take one wrong bite, they fall into the indulgent phase where there's no attempt to use willpower at all. They either have 100 per cent willpower or none. The perfect phase is often quite exciting, although there's usually some anxiety that it will end and about what will happen when it does.

The real problem with perfect eating, of course, is that it never can last. It's a very, very tall order to eat in a perfect way (whatever that means!) every day for the rest of your life. If you try to use willpower too rigidly with food, you'll stay in that same diet/binge pattern. And what usually happens then is that once you've blown it, you resist getting back on track because it means going back into that rigid state of perfection.

By far the best strategy is to aim to use willpower over food for a percentage of the time, rather than all the time. Take control of addictive overeating by degrees rather than completely, as when you eliminate perfect success you also eliminate perfect failure. Simply stop aiming for perfection. You don't need it. It's not perfection that leads you to succeed with willpower over food, it's gaining an acceptance of your addictive desire. When you have achieved that to a significant extent, then, even when you do eat addictively, you can easily get back into control.

Whenever you begin a challenge with willpower, it's best to face as much of the difficulty as you can from the start. Avoiding some of the difficult circumstances doesn't mean you are doomed to failure. *What leads you to fail is avoiding difficulty so that you never learn how to manage your addictive desire.*

Instead, you remain fearful of it and when it's there you fight it and pretend you have no choice. That's what causes failure with willpower.

Many people meet the difficulty of willpower and don't realise that there's a process of change involved which is going to take some time. They just think that this is too difficult and it's going to stay this way. They expect an instant break-through, and when it doesn't happen they look around for some gimmick or pill that will do it for them. It never happens all at once. If you think there should be an instant, magic solution this is an important point to grasp.

Step by Step

★ **Prioritise motivation to use willpower that benefits you –** as distinct from reasons to change your behaviour for the good of others or to please others. It may be that other people will benefit from your use of willpower, but it's crucial for you to know that you will benefit too.

★ **Ask yourself if you really do want to use willpower –** This may seem a strange step at this stage, but if you've spent some time with this book and it still isn't working for you, it's worth pointing out that motivation to use willpower is not guaranteed. It could be that your inability to use willpower comes from not having any intention of it. The notion that you don't have willpower could come from some vague sense that you 'should' change your ways, when in fact you don't really want to.

★ **Choose to persevere – or not!** – Whether or not you persevere is something you have a choice about as well. If you don't want to keep going, that's your choice. However, you can only make your choices in the present time, so don't try to predict or commit to persevering. Simply know that you'll be making choices as you go. If you incorporate what you've learned in this book, those choices will become easier to make as you go along.

★ **Work on overcoming learned helplessness and fear of failure** – by noticing anything that's different about this attempt to use willpower. Perhaps you're older and wiser. Perhaps some circumstance in your life has changed that could make a big difference. Perhaps, in the past, you didn't have all the necessary information in order to succeed, and perhaps this book is providing you with that information. Perhaps you didn't really want to succeed before because you had another agenda going, such as proving something to someone. It wasn't that you couldn't do it, it was just that failing was more important to you because it rewarded you in a different way. These circumstances may not apply now. If you can see these things, you can see the possibility of success with willpower this time.

★ **Re-evaluate pessimistic beliefs** – by finding positive ways to describe what's happening. Because it's new thinking it can seem false – but it's important not to lie. For example, if you think you're a failure at something, you could change it to: 'I just haven't done it yet.' This is every bit as true and will give you a very different feeling about it because it opens up the possibility of achieving it in the future. Use this principle in your thoughts and in your spoken language. Notice when you say things such as 'I'm hopeless at that' or 'I can't do it' or 'I'm useless' or 'I don't have any willpower.' It's easy to get into the habit of putting yourself down like this, but amazingly easy to get out of it. Just notice when you're talking or thinking like this – and stop!

★ **Be as honest as you can** – Affirmations are a tool often recommended for personal development and raising self-esteem, but they are not helpful when they are not based on the truth, which is so often advised. Affirming that you are healthy and slim when you are clearly neither is confusing and deceitful. Affirming that you are a wonderful dancer when you clearly have two left feet isn't helpful. What's better is to work towards accepting yourself unconditionally – warts and all, including the two left feet – and learning to celebrate what's real about you and what strengths you genuinely possess. From that position you can work towards making the changes that are possible. Self-esteem is strengthened whenever you tell the truth, or at least when you make your best efforts to discover the truth. For the same reason, it's best to tell the truth about addictive desire, so that, for example, you're honest with yourself that you really do want that second helping. Then you can manage that addictive hunger if you so choose. Rigorous honesty is astoundingly effective in creating change.

★ **Take Post-it notes or index cards and write prompts** – such as: 'Do I have to?' 'I can't?' 'I have a choice' and 'Should I?' and place them where you're likely to catch sight of them often. This will help you to become more aware of thoughts such as these whenever they cross your mind, in connection with absolutely anything. When you can catch them you can question them, and you'll find it's very rarely true that you 'have to' or 'can't'. The more you bring this new thinking into your life, the more you'll have a real sense of free choice when you want to use willpower. The bonus is that you'll be less of a victim/slave, and will gain greater mastery over your life in general.

★ **When you're under stress, find a way to stop, relax and take some time out** – It can be tough to think straight when you have too many things to do and too little time to do them. When you have so many demands and deadlines, the last thing you think you need to do is stop. Meditate. Go sit in the garden. Sing a song. Go for a walk. Do some gardening or whatever – but let your mind rest. Allow the panic to subside for a while and create, even very temporarily, a more peaceful state of mind. Get your mind off your problems and the solutions will begin to appear. What you've done is to create a space to hear your subconscious wisdom. You'll be able to see how to prioritise, and what can be delegated or renegotiated so that you don't need to do it at all. Relaxation – even for just a few moments – is the key. It will allow you to connect with the whole picture rather than obsessing over the details, and it may well save you more time than it took!

★ **Let go of 'all or none' thinking about food** – Think instead in terms of percentages, aiming for whatever percentage seems to work for you. This requires giving up the excitement of being in that perfect state. Whenever you notice your eating is 'perfect', make some deliberate errors. For example, eat something you would normally only eat when you're out of control. You'll lose the thrill of perfection, but you'll also lose the nightmare, out-of-control eating when it all falls apart.

Where There's a Will: Anne

Eating has been an issue all of my life. I am a woman of thirty-eight and I can remember feeling – and being – fat at six or seven. I enjoyed food and ate too much. I can remember being miserable and my mum trying to help me by telling me which foods were fattening and which weren't. Apparently that worked when she was a fat child but it didn't work for me.

At eighteen I starved myself until, for my height and frame, I was very thin. Then I yo-yoed for God knows how many years, going from twelve stone to sixteen to fourteen to eleven. I would have been happy at ten stone. I tried loads and loads of diets. Some were very successful in terms of weight loss but there was nothing I could hold on to and keep up for the rest of my life. I was feeling utterly desperate and out of control, and could easily have ended up at twenty-five stone, when I decided to give the 'Eating Less' seminars a shot.

Being encouraged to rethink what I was doing marked the beginning of change for me. Before, the only reason on earth to change my eating habits was to lose weight and be thin. I'm ashamed to say that I had got to thirty-eight, yet was still unable to work out that there were other benefits to eating less, such as feeling able and inclined to do something in the evening instead of just lying bloated and distended on the sofa! The first time I didn't eat at break time I felt such a sense of achievement and it had a massive impact on my self-esteem. As time went on I inevitably began to lose weight – and I was trying not to get excited about that!

I think the vital fact for me has been that I now see myself as having a choice. Before, I'd see myself as dieting or not dieting – and if I broke out of a diet there was no going back, I'd blown it. It was like being trapped in a box. You could break out of it or stay stuck in it, and you'd feel bad either way, in or out. Here there's no box. You make your choice every time for everything you think about eating. You eat it – or you don't. You decide to eat just so much – or you don't. There is no forever decision.

I still feel my addictive desire and I've found it terribly important to be aware of it. Before I'd spend my time trying to avoid confronting it – all that stuff about not having 'bad' foods around and keeping sticks of carrot and celery in the fridge to suppress the urge with, which never works anyway, of course. Now I know the biscuits are there, I know I want one, I know I don't need one and I make my choice. Although I still feel addictive desire, it is much more fleeting now. Sometimes it passes really quickly. In every ten times I experience it, I probably give in to it only once.

The biggest thing I've got out of all this is that I can safely say I am not actually frightened of food any more. It can get the better of me sometimes but it doesn't faze me. The fact that I'm not perfect about food and yet I still feel relaxed about it is the best thing I could imagine feeling. What I've found is that I'm happier now than I've ever been in my life.

Notes

1. One of the biggest myths is that cigarettes are relaxing and calming for smokers. Studies have shown that not only do smokers have higher levels of anxiety in general, but that smoking often pre-dates problems such as panic attacks, agoraphobia and depression, strongly suggesting that smoking could be part of the cause of these conditions (*New Scientist*, April 2002).

'...numerous laboratory studies have failed to detect any mood enhancing effects of smoking or nicotine.' In comparisons with nicotine-free cigarettes, normal cigarettes have been found to produce a 'mild stimulant effect' only. *Nicotine Addiction in Britain*, Report of the Tobacco Advisory Group of the Royal College of Physicians, 2000.

As for overeating, the recent 'Food and Mood' study conducted by the mental health charity Mind found that 80 per cent experienced significant improvement with depression, panic attacks and anxiety by cutting down on sugar. Caffeine, alcohol and chocolate were also found to make a difference, and a quarter of those in the survey said that their mood swings, depression or anxiety had disappeared.

2. See Nathaniel Branden's *The Six Pillars of Self-Esteem* (Bantam, 1994).

3. One of these studies was published in the journal *Addiction* (97, 87–93, 2001), 'The urge to smoke depends on the expectation of smoking'.

A study published in the *British Medical Journal* (July 2002) says that smoking among employees falls significantly when offices and other workplaces become smoke-free zones, with many people encouraged to cut back or stop altogether. Other studies of the effects of smoke-free environments in America, Australia, Canada and Germany found that the number of smokers fell by 4 per cent in an average period of ten months. The effectiveness of no-smoking policies is why the tobacco industry is so keen to stop them being introduced. It is estimated that, if all workplaces were smoke-free, cigarette consumption in Britain would fall by over 7 per cent, costing the tobacco industry £310 million a year.

4. 'Narcotic use in Southeast Asia and afterward', published in *Archives of General Psychiatry* (32;955–961).

5. Two studies mentioned in the *Annual Review of Public Health* (1994; 15:345–366) estimate an 85 per cent risk of returning to full-time smoking after one 'lapse'.

CHAPTER EIGHT

Willpower at Last

Staying motivated

We jump at the sight of a snake, even though it's in a cage in a zoo. We developed this survival instinct at a time when snakes were real dangers to us. What the evolutionary process has not been able to develop, however, are instincts for avoiding the dangers we encounter now, such as fast food, cigarettes and drugs. In time, our species may cope much better with them, but that's not going to make any impact on us and our lives today. Meanwhile, we simply cannot rely on our survival instincts because they can't even begin to alert us to the dangers we face.

In the not too distant past it would have been a wonderful idea to eat whatever we wanted, whenever we were hungry and to stop when we were full. Our natural desires would have been to meet our natural needs with natural food – and, naturally, we would have walked a few miles to get at it! These days, however, the only thing we can rely on is our ability to think.

This is why we need willpower, more than ever before. Without it change is not possible except on superficial levels. With willpower, we can transform our lives, survive and even thrive in this bizarre environment in which we now live.

Simply begin by catching the automatic thought of desire. Get used to noticing it when it's there. Knowing that this is simply the memory of something you did in the past enables you to accept the inevitability of it and it allows you to forgive yourself for thinking this way. Your desire is just a memory and that's all. You just did it in the past and that's all. It doesn't mean you're a bad person or that you have some deep psychological, genetic or biochemical problem to overcome.

Maybe in the past you didn't know any better. Maybe circumstances were such that this addiction looked like a good option. The problem is that the circumstances can change but the addiction tends to stick. That's why you need willpower.

When willpower is described as powerful free will you can see that it's a choice, so there's no way you can't have any. Using willpower means choosing what seems at the time to be the more difficult or uncomfortable alternative. You may not have been making those choices in the past and you might not make those choices ever – *but this doesn't mean you don't have the ability to do it.* It may be that you want willpower but you're not willing to do what it takes. You want willpower but only if it's easy and effortless. You want willpower but without paying the price of time, effort, attention and allowing yourself to feel unsatisfied at times.

It's possible to go through life with no attempt to use willpower at all. You can place a high value on self-indulgence, identifying yourself with it and thinking of it as an asset. But if you persistently act on impulse only to regret it later, this is a clue that there's something about your way of life that doesn't work for you. You'll have ways to explain these actions to yourself, justifying them with some circumstance, past or present. But when you look closer, and especially when you begin to change your ways, you could discover that a great deal more was affected by not using willpower than you had realised.

It could be that you don't know how good things can be when you use willpower to make changes in your life. *When you can begin to see the possibilities, you connect with your motivation to change.*

Understanding Motivation

If you don't have much interest in making changes you're obviously not going to bother. Before you can make any changes at all, you need to have some idea of what it is you want to create in your life. Becoming and staying motivated can be tricky, though, so here are some thoughts about how elusive inspiration can be – especially during those moments of addictive desire – and what to do about it.

Delayed rewards

The closer a reward is to the effort that earns it, the more rewarding it seems to be and the easier it is to stay motivated. After all, if you were training a dog to fetch your slippers, you would reward the dog immediately, wouldn't you? If the dog brought your slippers, it wouldn't make any sense to pat him on the head and say 'Good dog!' two weeks later.

This is why it can be tough to get excited about using willpower at first. On one hand, the rewards of *not* using will-power are instant. On the other hand, when you start to use willpower your rewards take time to show up.

This is a particular problem when it comes to overeating, because so many people try to motivate themselves to change their appearance, which can be a slow and erratic process, as you may know. It will help you a great deal to identify *any bene-fit you experience* from taking control of overeating, such as more energy, improved mood and a sense of accomplishment. Most overeaters feel improvements such as these within two days of changing their eating habits, long before any fat is lost. These benefits need to be deliberately remembered, though, so that they can continue to motivate you, no matter what size you are.

Although some of your rewards may be fairly rapid, some may take a very long time indeed, so it's still crucial to take the reality of delayed rewards into consideration. Who says you should get your rewards immediately anyway? Most people don't think their boss should shove money in their hands after every half-hour at work. So why not be content to wait for your rewards with willpower, just as you wait for your pay cheque at the end of the month?

Possibly the most significant rewards are those that are the most delayed: an active and youthful old age, free from pain, disease and disability. Many people miss this potential motivation. For example, I've heard a recent survey quoted in various places, where people were asked if they would change their lifestyle in order to live an extra year. Half of the 1,020 polled said that if told to give up cigarettes, change their diet or take up exercise in exchange for living twelve months longer, they'd stick with their bad habits. However, the question is seriously misleading. Instead, people should have been asked if they wanted to spend the last ten, twenty or thirty years of their lives in as good health, as fit and active, as when they were young.

If you keep in mind that an ounce of prevention is worth a ton of cure, you won't wait for disaster to strike before you start to make changes. It's never too late, even if you already have symptoms of serious health problems.

Emphasis on the positive

As we saw in Chapter Two, you can motivate yourself by enticing yourself with positive rewards (better health, money saved and increased self-esteem) or by frightening yourself with negative consequences (symptoms of ill health, debt, guilt and lower self-esteem). They are flip sides of the same coin.

By all means remind yourself of both positive and negative, but in general it's better to encourage yourself with improvements rather than to intimidate yourself with threats. Thinking along the lines of 'don't you dare do that or there'll be hell to pay' tends to reinforce low self-esteem and the slave attitude of restricting and denying oneself. On the other hand, trading the feeling of addictive desire for an improved quality of life is an entirely positive and powerful way to make a choice.

Choose what to value

An extraordinarily successful programme was developed by a clinic treating inner-city cocaine addicts in the USA:[1] every time an addict came into the centre and tested negative for drug use, they were paid money. The payments started at a couple of dollars and increased for each consecutive time they tested clean. The centre, which normally expects 70 per cent to have dropped out of the programme within the first six weeks, found that a spectacular 85 per cent stayed with the programme for twelve weeks and 70 per cent stayed for six months! It makes sense, doesn't it? The problem was that it was considered inappropriate to pay people to obey the law and take care of their own health. So it was tough for the clinic to generate the necessary funds from the government and health insurers.

What we can learn from this is that addiction is overcome when the costs of continuing are outweighed by the benefits of quitting. How do you know when the costs outweigh the benefits? This depends on nothing other than your re-evaluation of your priorities. *Success with willpower simply depends on what you choose to value.*

It may be that you've already made these kinds of choices in your life. For example, an overeater who wouldn't even try to use willpower in private may not have any difficulty at all when dining with her in-laws. Some smokers quit when they become parents or develop relationships with non-smokers. Many parents will use willpower to move mountains for their children while ignoring their own needs, every day, in a host of different ways. This is all about what they choose to value.

A recent newspaper article tells the story of an obese woman who, after struggling with her weight for over twenty years, lost four stone in six months when she needed to donate one of her kidneys to save her son's life. The doctors wouldn't risk operating on her unless she lost the weight, and she writes that every time she felt tempted to eat she thought of her son and 'found the willpower I never knew I had'.

She ends the article by saying that not only has her son got a new lease of life but she now feels like a new person, 'fit and full of go'. So hopefully she will continue to motivate herself for more 'selfish' benefits now that the operations are behind them.

You could wait for outside circumstances to change. You could wait for someone to come along and pay you to use willpower. Or you could re-evaluate your priorities instead. What will you choose to value? Make self-esteem your priority and you'll have a vital key in motivating yourself to use will-power. You need to value yourself – and if you find that tough to do, you fake it until it starts to become a reality. Whenever your self-esteem takes a beating, as it undoubtedly will from time to time, that's when your willpower becomes vulnerable. But this is exactly when using willpower will bring you your most powerful rewards because it helps to restore self-esteem.

Motivation isn't a feeling

If you aren't getting the results you want, it may be because you have chosen to use willpower only when you feel like it. It's not because you are incapable of it. You just chose something else. You chose to do it only when you were in the mood for it. When you see you have a choice, then you see that you can change your choice.

If you use willpower only when you feel like it, this will

only take you so far. It's using willpower when you *don't* feel like it that turns failure into success.

It's almost guaranteed that you won't connect with the passion behind your goals all the time – especially during moments of addictive desire and especially when your self-esteem is low. But you can at least remember that there is a light at the end of the tunnel, even when you can't actually see it!

An Inspiring Way to Live

No matter how productive our lives are, most of us develop routines, eating the same kinds of food, having the same kinds of conversations, doing the same kinds of things over and over. These routines become so familiar that we often assume this is how life must be. And when we look around us, everybody else is probably doing the same, so we think it's inevitable. Anything too different is for 'other people' and certainly not anyone we know. On some level, though, there's often some-thing a bit boring about life like this, so every now and then we feel like breaking out by doing something wild. But is the 'something wild' nothing but pure indulgence? Is the way you break life's monotony some kind of addictive excess? More addictive food, drugs, booze, shopping, gambling or what-ever? And, worst of all, are you doing it more and more frequently, so that it's now turned into its own boring routine?

There's another way to break out of these ruts that we all settle into and love and hate in equal measure – and that's by setting the right kinds of challenges for yourself. When life seems a bit dull, it's a sure sign we aren't challenging ourselves enough. Our spirits thrive on challenge and when we ignore this truth we create misery for ourselves. There is another way to live, however, and it has a completely different quality to it, one which nurtures this special human quality of spirit and creativity.

It needs to be the right kind of challenge, though, because many of us are happy to face challenges in some areas of our lives while fearful of others. You may already face plenty of challenges at work but evade them in your relationships with your family. You may be facing the challenge of keeping fit but keep all your time filled, avoiding your challenge of relaxation and time alone. You may cope well with the daily challenge of bringing up children but use that to excuse your indulgence with food or cigarettes.

You may resist the idea of taking on anything more, but facing new challenges, *provided this is done correctly*, makes things better, not worse. You can discover that replacing self-indulgence with self-control, far from leaving you more vulnerable, leads to a much greater capacity to cope with life and a more positive outlook in general. This is the gift of stronger self-esteem.

As we've seen, addiction exploits the natural reward system

we have that encourages us to support our lives. In order to break free from addiction we need to pay attention to a different kind of reward system, one that's just as essential to our humanity and just as powerful. This is the reward system of self-esteem.

When facing a willpower challenge, you don't start out with the highest level of self-esteem, and you don't start out feeling confident of success. All you start out with is a bit of hope – and you build on that. You consider that real, lasting change *might* be possible, even though you have no past experience to support that notion. But when you're hopeful and you're working towards your chosen goal, you've moved out of a vicious circle and are starting to build a positive, self-reinforcing circle based on the possibility of change. In the process, you start to build a deep respect for yourself and an acknowledgement and honouring of your worth as a human being. It could be that the more you fear and resist making a particular change, the more rewarding it will be when you do.

The truth is that you already have willpower and you use it every day. It may seem so normal and obvious in some regards that you don't even question it, yet others will find some of the things you do extremely daunting. All you need to develop is the willpower to make the changes you want to make. By facing temptation, and your fears about it, you don't have to follow your automatic patterns – and you can still feel like a winner instead of a loser. It takes courage. It's challenging. And it's an inspiring way to live.

Step by Step

★ **Return to this book every now and then** – After you've read the book, come back to it later on and you will understand things in a new way and see things you hadn't seen before. This is because you will have had some time to become more aware of the process, and you'll still be on a learning curve and ready for more.

★ **Eat for optimum health** – No matter what addictive behaviour you are trying to control, build up your natural ability to manufacture your own mood-enhancing neurotransmitters by eating lean protein, essential fats, whole grains, fruit and vegetables. This style of eating is less likely to become addictive because it won't deliver the same highs and lows, but will certainly improve general mood levels and bring down anxiety and stress. It's also possible that it will contribute to a milder experience of withdrawal, for example, when quitting smoking.

★ **Exercise for optimum health** – Higher levels of serotonin, dopamine and endorphins are produced when we take exercise of any kind. And exercise reduces stress by helping to eliminate the stress hormones adrenalin and cortisol. Exercise increases mental clarity by bringing more blood to the brain. Studies have shown that older people who exercise regularly do as well at mental tests as others who are thirty or forty years younger.

★ **Use what you've learned** – Will isn't just about thinking. At some point action needs to be taken. It's not enough to understand the ideas in this book while you're reading it. The only thing that will make a difference is to use them in those moments when you need willpower.

★ **Go for it** – You just might reach the goals you are setting out to achieve!

Where There's a Will: Zoe

I had my last drink six weeks ago, which is not a long time but it's a first for me. My partner still has the odd beer, but doesn't bring it home, and I'm sure he'll eventually stop altogether as well. I found myself taking some absurd risks by driving after too many cocktails. I've been reading this book in manuscript, and it has been terrific inspiration. There have been times when I've thought I'd just have one glass of wine or something, and I made a choice. I'm not saying I'll never have another drink. For now, though, it's what I'm choosing.

The big learning for me is that choice doesn't last. All I can do is to choose for now and later on choose for now again. So many people think they choose for ever when they give something up, but you just can't do that.

I met my current partner eight months ago, we fell in love almost immediately and had the most indescribably wonderful times together, all heavily under the influence. However, remarkably soon we started to get aggressive and bitter towards each other, even though we still felt very attracted. We would drink and we would fight, and we started doing this within about six weeks of getting together.

One thing this book has helped me realise is that the change in my personality when I drink, which I've always known is quite dramatic, is a cover-up for my low self-esteem. Outwardly, I'm fun and strong and smart and capable, but it's all an act that masks the inner self-loathing that nobody else even begins to suspect. Now that I've seen this, I doubt I'll ever return to the level of drinking I used to do because I just can't con myself about it any more.

I love the clarity of mind I have now and I especially love not wasting time with all those hangovers. I'm glad to be free from the anxiety of wondering whether or not I'm legal when I drive. My relationship is so good it's frightening. I think to go through the process of not drinking is great discipline. It's a warm-up for some of the more subtle exercises with willpower.

Notes

1. Reported in *New Scientist* September 1994. A report in the journal *Addictive Behaviors* (2002; 27, 887–910) gives an overview

of a number of studies of voucher-based incentives for substance abuse treatment, including a successful programme aimed at pregnant, low-income smokers. At the end of the pregnancy, 32 per cent were not smoking compared to 9 per cent in a control group. After two months with the new baby, 21 per cent were still not smoking compared with 6 per cent in the control group.

FURTHER READING

On self-esteem:

The Six Pillars of Self-Esteem, Nathaniel Branden, PhD (Bantam, 1994)

On stopping smoking:

How To Stop Smoking and Stay Stopped For Good, Gillian Riley (Vermilion, 1992)

On taking control of overeating:

Eating Less: Take Control of Overeating, Gillian Riley (Vermilion, 1999)

On the biochemistry of health and nutrition:

From Here To Longevity, Mitra Ray, PhD (self-published, 2002, only available at www.fromheretolongevity.com)

On overcoming panic attacks and phobias:

Triumph Over Fear, Jerilyn Ross, MA (Bantam, 1994)

On brain rehabilitation:

Mind Sculpture, Ian Robertson (Bantam, 1999)

On the power and biology of belief:

Timeless Healing, Herbert Benson, MD (Simon & Schuster, 1996)

On the latest breakthroughs in research and medicine:

Medicine Today (monthly, by subscription: call 020 7435 8253 or email sales@medicine-today.co.uk)

FURTHER HELP

Gillian Riley is a counsellor and seminar leader who has been helping people to take control of smoking and overeating addictions since 1982. A former smoker and overeater, she brings to her work an understanding of the process of addiction gained through counselling others and through dealing with her own addictive behaviour.

For information on 'Eating Less' courses, led by Gillian Riley, send an email via the www.eatingless.com web site.

ALSO AVAILABLE FROM VERMILION BY GILLIAN RILEY

Eating Less	0091826152	£7.99
How to Stop Smoking and Stay Stopped for Good	0091887763	£5.99

FREE POSTAGE AND PACKING
Overseas customers allow £2.00 per paperback

ORDER:

By phone: 01624 677237

By post: Random House Books
c/o Bookpost
PO Box 29
Douglas
Isle of Man IM991BQ

By fax: 01624 670923

By email: bookshop@enterprise.net

Cheques (payable to Bookpost) and credit cards accepted

Prices and availability subject to change without notice.
Allow 28 days for delivery.
When placing your order, please mention if you do
not wish to receive any additional information.

www.randomhouse.co.uk